THE
5%
ZONE

Visibility Strategies to Get you Recognized and Rewarded in Any Organization

STEPHEN KREMPL

For more information contact:
Krempl Communications International LLC

Singapore – Singapore Office
9 Raffles Place #58-01
Singapore 048619

USA – Issaquah Office
1567 Highlands Dr NE, Suite 110-188
Issaquah, WA 98029

Website: http://www.KremplCommunications.com

Disclaimer: Krempl Communications International LLC reserves the right to revise this publication and make changes from time to time in its content without notice.

Endorsements for Stephen Krempl and his GEM Training

Stephen's book "The 5% Zone" and the accompanying online program is what participants need to excel in the work world. Coupled with an engaging style and great information, Stephen helps excites on the secrets on being visible in the work world.

James Malinchak
Featured on ABC's Hit TV Show," Secret Millionaire
Co-Author, Chicken Soup for the College Soul
Two time National Speaker of the Year
Founder, www.BigMoneySpeaker.com

"Stephen, thank you for being the keynote speaker at the official launch of our HQ – Krempl partnership in Cairo and the Gulf. We received amazing feedback for the entire event, and everyone loved your GEM message. Also, I like to say your energy and passion in which you delivered it made a huge difference. "

Sally Shaheen, PHR , MBA.
Co-Founder and Managing Director at Human Quality

Your high energy and humorous yet direct style of presentation on our webinar captured the full attention of our participants. We know this because we noticed the participant numbers kept growing to 400+, with no one dropping out. Also, the evaluations and overwhelming questions we received during Q & A, showed us the content was right on target, insightful, and really valuable.

Tammy Lee
Talent Development, Global Business Services,
Asia Pacific, BASF

"I first met Stephen Krempl as a training professional in Singapore in 1992 and have enjoyed working closely with him on important projects. Stephen is one of the first Asian-born members of the global training community to rise to the highest levels with multi-national companies based in the USA, including becoming the Chief Learning Officer of Starbucks in Seattle, Washington.

Ron Kaufman, Founder, UP! Your Service

"I was wondering about how to inject one of my staff with more self-confidence in dealing with clients. When I enrolled her in the GEM program, I had hoped for improvement but was not expecting the kind of transformation she underwent. She came back with so much more confidence and is now much more comfortable with interacting with clients than before. GEM has helped her significantly—I plan to send more of my team to learn the GEM skills."

**Lai Kwok Kin, Managing Director,
WeR1 Consultants Pte Ltd.
(Investor Relations Agency based in Singapore)**

I recommend his outstanding GEM workshop. Not only is Stephen an engaging presenter, but also the content on developing executive skills for a globalized corporate world is both relevant and highly effective.

**James Reinnoldt
University of Washington
Lecturer of Managerial Communications and
Global Business**

"In all my years providing OD and leadership development solutions to client groups, I rank GEM (Global Executive Mindset) training as a true game changer for our staff. GEM is a key enabler of our strategy to accelerate the readiness of our talent to step in key business roles. They have increased their visibility to Senior stakeholders internally in their home country as well as at the international level.

Isabelle Claus Teixeira
ALCON, Asia & Japan Head of Talent management and OD

We have worked in partnership with Krempl Communications to develop our employees to a new level. We found the Global Executive Mindset (GEM) program to be of great benefit to our employees and it has consequently improved employee interaction, participation and confidence within our global organization. From employee feedback and subsequent management assessment, the effectiveness of GEM has been significant and we fully intend to continue to run this program.

Gary McIntosh
Human Resources Manager CB&I

We used the GEM/W3 programs for all our graduate trainees. It was a clear content differentiator for the graduates of our program. The content provided students with key information and the all-important practice on how to Standout and Win in the Work World. To date, 1800 students have successfully gone through the program and it has made a difference in their ability to communicate confidently as they move into their careers.

Haji Zuber Moud Isa,
Founder / Managing Director
BriTay Asia (M) Sdn Bhd

"The GEM online program has really improved my confidence and provided me the tools on how to stand out especially when connecting with higher levels. At my one-on-one session with my Manager last Friday, I used the "set up statement" technique and she was impressed. Then when our program director was onsite, I was able to confidently introduce myself and started a conversation using FORM, something I would never do in the past."

Merlin M, RN, BSN
Health Care Professional

"Stephen's ability to quickly and thoroughly assess any business's education and training requirements is not only unique but invaluable. His specialty of designing and facilitating training to address those needs across multiple cultures whether in Asia, the U.S., or the Middle East is well known amongst clients and professionals."

Blair Singer, Co-author of *SALES DOG*

"We have seen Stephen work at every level in the corporate environment and he brings a special brilliance, unique insights, and immense experience when working with leaders, managers, and all stakeholders in an organization. Therefore, he is a catalyst for problem solving, change, and learning aimed at organizational results."

Gaylan W. Nielson, CEO,
The Work Itself Group, Co-author of *FAKE WORK*

"I have known Stephen for 20 years. His personal qualities and experience at senior levels of global multinationals have given him a special understanding of the dynamics in many cultures— be it in Asia, the U.S., or the Middle East. Coupled with his unique facilitation skills, this makes him perfectly placed to inspire Asians to success in the global world."

Philip Merry, Founder/CEO,
Global Leadership Academy

"Stephen has been doing work with us in the Middle East for many years. Whether it was delivering training or consulting on several high level projects, he has always been able to "connect" with our organization, our staff and our partners, bringing his corporate experience and his global experience."

**Mohamed Farouk Hafeez, Exec. VP HR,
Kuwait Food Company (Americana)**

"Stephen Krempl's dynamic, upbeat tempo, facilitation skills and message captured the attention of an audience of our senior leaders in a recent meeting in Houston... a powerful lively demonstration provided everyone with a memorable experience. His skill at working with and engaging the audience made his presentation fun and entertaining."

Ray Vigil, former CLO Humana Inc

"Everyone I've talked to stated that the information was useful and most of all NOT BORING! Your presentation was a large part of that along with your ability to teach and have fun at the same time."

—Scott Barry, Vice President of People Development

"I have been a student of Stephen's for a long time and am amazed by his ability to convert concepts to clear learning and practice. Every time he works with a group he is able to connect with them, excite them into learning, and most importantly, always leave an impact on his students. I have seen this happen many times as he facilitated his GEM workshops for our clients in Malaysia, Indonesia, China, and across Asia. He is a true Guru of the 5% Zone."

Prim Farim, Founder of Dibtagroup

Table of Contents

Preface

Pretend you're the HR manager for a major multinational organization, and you're about to make a critical hire. You've narrowed the field down to two candidates. Here are a few excerpts from their recommendation letters below:

Candidate #1
He worked hard.
He was always on time.
He rose to executive level after 8 years.

Candidate #2
He made a real difference in our organization.
Just one of his ideas changed our business for the better.
Our CEO took notice of him after their first online meeting.

Which one stands out, candidate #1 or #2? Chances are you didn't have to think about the answer for long. Candidate #2 is the obvious choice. Now, there's nothing wrong with Candidate #1. He appears to be a normal and consistent employee. But if you're reading this right now, I bet that's not what you want people to say about you. You want to be remembered and you want to stand out and be visible.

If you're not VISIBLE you are INVISIBLE

I also assume you are good at what you do and have the right attitude to match. Well guess what? You get a few first shots and even fewer second chances, and bear in mind you have plenty of smart colleagues and even more experienced ones who are all vying for the recognition and promotions that you want for yourself.

The bottom line is this: The one who stands out on the job the best gets remembered. You are fighting to stand out from the com- petition and increase your chances of getting promoted or receiving the positive nod from your peers and supervisors. Your com- petition is anyone who comes before you or after you, especially when several people are pitching their ideas, projects, or points of view at the same meeting or business review. So in order to stand out, you must articulate your point of view more effectively or do your job better than the person who came before you or the one who comes after you.

Are you willing to make the effort to stand out, connect, and communicate better than your competition? Well, you've already made a positive first step. By investing in this book, you now have access to some special insights that much of your competition just doesn't know about. What is it that sets the special people apart from the pack? How can you stand out? You will discover how to stand out and be remembered in the pages that follow as you learn all about the 5% Zone and the five situations where you can make the most difference.

We also like to share with you how we developed the GEM Model. The original research came from interviewing one hundred executives from different companies and industries to ask them what more they wanted from their managers and leaders.

From these interviews and my own experience within the companies I worked in and consulted for, is where we developed the GEM model (**see page 83**) Here is the demographical data for the interviewees: -

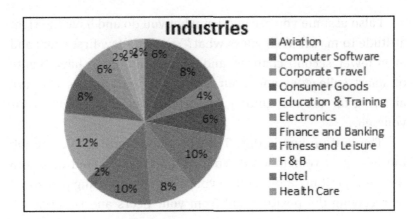

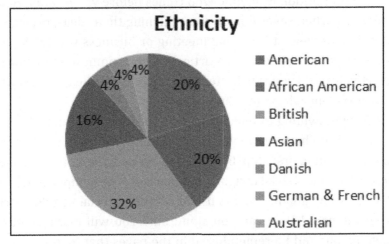

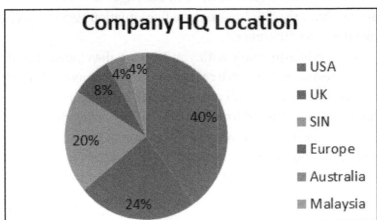

Introduction

Introduction

I am Stephen Krempl the CEO of Krempl Communications International. As an international trainer, speaker, author, and coach, I have worked with thousands of leaders in over 30+ countries. My career spanned 25 years working for Fortune 500 companies, **Starbucks Coffee Company**, where I was Chief Learning Officer (Seattle), **YUM Brands Inc**. VP of Yum University and Global Learning (Louisville), **PepsiCo** Restaurants International, Director (Dallas), and **Motorola,** Regional Manager (Singapore), where I had a front row seat to see why some employees excelled and why others did not.

My goal is to help individuals develop their skills so that they can stand out, get noticed and advance their careers in their corporations, even in this increasingly competitive global marketplace of ours. I have authored several books, but this is my favorite: **The 5% Zone: Visibility Strategies that will Get you Recognized and Rewarded in Any Organization.**

In this book, I teach the same concepts and techniques from my Growing Executive Mindsets (GEM) programs, which are presented as keynotes speeches, in house workshops and online programs around the world. We have conducted this for various groups within many global organizations; leaders and high potentials, employee resource groups, engineers, finance, HR, government relations, etc. or numerous managers who aspire to become better leaders and get noticed within their organizations. For more information, go to:www.kremplcommunications.com.

Why this book?

I created my programs and wrote this book because I was sick and tired of seeing my colleagues bypassed for promotion, or the critical project lead position they wanted or just getting recognition from senior management. It was not because they were not smart, hardworking, or loyal, but many of them hid behind this thought (actually excuse) – " Stephen, my work will speak for itself" or worst still "I am an introvert, I not good at speaking up."

Well, I am an introvert as well – I hate talking to people, but that doesn't mean I don't know how to do it and do it well when I need to. It's like when my wife says, "Hon, the Smiths are coming over for dinner," I go "Really, can't we have dinner by ourselves?" But, when the Smiths come over, I am engaged, and I make sure everyone is having a great time. We talk and laugh although being my best for our dinner guests – is hard work (for me).

I am going to ask you three questions, you must answer with either a yes or no answer, I don't want the" well it depends," so here we go:

Does the Smartest person always get noticed or promoted?
YES or NO

Does the Hardest working person always get noticed or promoted?
YES or NO

Does the most Loyal person always get noticed or promoted?
YES or NO

If you answered NO, then you answered the same way as my participants would respond when I speak or train with audiences around the world. My real question to you is:

What gets a person noticed or promoted in your organization?

I ask this question and give participants a chance to do a quick discussion with the person sitting next to them. The response I get is usually wide-ranging (actually pandemonium breaks out), many shake their heads, some laugh, others' sigh, and others utter some choice words under their breath, you get the idea. The point is not that smarts, hard work, and loyalty are not important; those are a given, but what are the other criteria that make you visible in your organization, and it may differ slightly from company to company and it will become even more important if you work remotely. I will mention it several more times in the book:

If you are not **Visible**, then you are **Invisible**.

Why be Visible

Now, I know you know this; the larger the organization, function, or group, the easier it is to hide. Conversely, opportunities in those large organizations or if you work remotely to get noticed are also correspondingly scarcer. In those corporations, you will have many more peers at the same level (especially if you are in a large global corporation), and many want to get noticed.

So, there is no shortage of competition and more reason for you to be ready when the opportunities appear.

You see, senior leaders talk about their business all the time. They also spend time talking about their future leaders and who is "up and coming." What do you think your senior leaders would say about you if I mentioned your name to them?

What would you want your senior leaders to say? Here are some possible responses: -

A) My question: "What do you think of Stephanie Lee?"

Leader's Response: "You know Stephanie is a solid worker, but you know she just seems a little hesitant to share her points of view, and when she does, she is always qualifying herself – seems like she is hedging her answers all the time."

Or

B) My question: "What do you think of Stephanie Lee?"

Leader's Response: "You know Stephanie she attends all the meetings, and she even sits upfront, but you know, she is mostly quiet at the meetings, I never quite know what's on her mind."

Or

C) My Question: "What do you think of Stephanie Lee?"

Leader's Response: "We all love Stephanie, she always adds value to a meeting, and she knows how to articulate her points of view clearly and succinctly – I think she will go far.

So, which response would you prefer - C, of course? Now those are the responses you may get if you participate and are visible in those meetings. If you are the type that will shy away from participating, then the answer may go like this: -

D) My Question: "What do you think of Stephanie Lee?"

Leader's Response: Stephanie, who? Who are you talking about?

If they don't even know your name – I am sorry to say, if that is your situation, you're out of luck. Now I am not suggesting you are like that, but can you imagine how bad that would look if they don't even recognize your name?

One more point, I must bring up, because many of you may not even realize this is happening. Here is my experience in many organizations, both those I have worked in and those I work with currently. When you are making a business presentation or just pitching an idea to senior management, they will say, "Great job Ryan we need more people like you with ideas like that in our organization."   You smile, you are happy, and when you leave the room or the call – then the leaders turn to each other and say,

"Well, that wasn't very good." Did Ryan hear that? NO, he heard, "Great job, we need more people like you." And then he wondered why he got bypassed for promotion.

You see, it's not what they say when you are in the room, it's what they say when you leave the room. Do you know what your senior leaders are saying about you after you leave the room? If you do great, if you don't, you better find out. All I want to do is increase your probability of success by using the ideas, techniques, and tips that you will find in the upcoming chapters.

Why 5%

Many people ask me why only 5%, well, unless your role requires you to meet or converse with senior management often as part of your work, for most others, you have much fewer opportunities. Its only 5% of the time that you will meet or call in with someone who is at least two levels above you or higher other than your current boss or supervisor.

What I want to share with you in this book is how you can use the many simple and actionable ideas in your 5% situations to create a more significant impact for yourself when these situations appear next. You will get a chance to plan and answer questions within the chapters to get you ready.

The 5 Situations

Also, we like to emphasize that there are only five situations that your senior leaders see or hear you. These are the five: -
1) your one-on-one meetings,
2) the team meetings, (small functional or the bigger town halls or all-hands meetings),
3) the conferences calls,
4) the business presentations, and
5) the company socials.

And, even if you work remotely, these apply – you will have one on one calls, team calls, possible larger call-ins, online presentations and social chats with individuals before the call formally starts that you still need to prepare.

And some of you are going, "Company socials, really?" – "Yes?" How good are you at talking to anyone about anything? Can you effortlessly join a group of senior leaders and participate in their conversation or talk about a non-work topic on a call with your senior managers? Well, we will show you a formula in **Part III, The GEM Differentiator** that you could use to make it easy on yourself. The reason it is crucial is most senior leaders are very comfortable speaking at "socials." It could be at lunches, pre-dinner receptions, pre call chat or just in the hallway, it is part of their role, and more importantly, they can tell if you are comfortable or not. So, if you aspire to be a senior leader, you better get good at this.

What do they remember about you when your name comes up? Were you quiet, or talked too much (also a problem) or were negative or complaining? What do you think will be the first memory that will pop in their head if you were complaining at the townhall – you guessed it "You mean Sam who's always complaining in our townhalls?" Look, they don't know if you came in at 7.30 am or left at 9.30 pm every evening. They remember their last interaction with you in those five situations in person or remotely.

So, I hope you know why you need these skills that I am sharing here in the book. I will be revealing some practical ideas, techniques and tips on how you can get even better at communicating confidently, connecting personally, and standing out. If you've decided, you need to be more visible in your organization then - let's keep going.

"95% of the time you can be who you are, but for the times you need to stand out you have to switch to your 5% Zone."

— STEPHEN KREMPL

Part I

WHAT IS THE 5% ZONE?

Our Philosophy

In part one of the book we are going to introduce you to our core GEM philosophies, your mindset required to succeed, the seven GEM behaviors and your approach.

You must understand and adopt these four core philosophies before you launch further into the book. It is essential that you recognize and embrace these philosophies, then you will understand why the skills, techniques, and tips that you will find in the rest of the book are needed.

95/5

The first thing you need to embrace is 95% of the time you just be yourself; I can't change you, and you don't really want to change, so let's not pretend. However, 5% of the time and remember this is with individuals two levels above you or higher, you must change the way you communicate and how you come across.

Why, because at this level there is an expectation that, you know how to articulate your points of view clearly, you can get to the point without wasting their time, and when challenged, you are confident enough to stand your ground and answer at least neutrally or positively.

Some people will go "Well, Stephen, that is not being "authentic." Yes, you are authentic within your "role." Just recognize you change your behavior and act differently on many occasions. Let me describe these different situations and let me know if you realize that your behavior changes in each of them.

1) When you are in the office, you behave in one way.

2) Then when you are out partying with your university/ college buddies, do you behave the same as when you are in the office?

3) When you go to your mother-in-law's house, do you act the same as you were with your buddies?

4) When you are supporting your favorite team – are you not going crazy when they score?

5) If you go to a place of worship – you act appropriately there - right?

You see, you change all the time. So, what makes you think you don't have to button up your communication style and your presence when you deal with senior management?

Good vs. Great

In our workshops, we all go through the concept of GOOD vs. GREAT. Here is where I have seen many people in organizations stop short because they thought they were already GOOD at what they did. However, my question is, are you GREAT at what you do? And, more importantly, does senior management think you are great or just good like everyone else?

The difference between good and great is making that decision to be great. Why? Because if you are just happy with being good, then you will not adopt any of the ideas, techniques, or tips that you will come across in this book – because "it is too much work" (in a winey voice).

All I can tell you is most senior management put a lot of work in preparation and becoming great at their craft; they just don't tell you. The best sports people in the world practice, and if they are the best, they probably practice more than their rivals. So, here is a question for you, if you think you want to become GREAT – how much time have you taken to practice communicating confidently, connecting personally, and standing out? I guarantee your answer will be – not quite enough. If you want to be visible and noticed in your organization, you have first to DECIDE you want to be great.

Rules of the Game

In every organization, there are rules that they would like their staff to operate, behave, and achieve results. Some of them are the written rules, and some are unwritten rules. Let me ask you, which are more important the written or the unwritten rules? Correct, Now here is the question, what are the rules of the game for your boss' boss? Are they the same for online versus face to face interactions?

Now, why focus on that person, because that is the one who will usually determine if you are ready for the next level.

I remember once when I just joined the organization, I was bringing up the name of my staff to my supervisor for promotion and she said: -

Supervisor: "No I don't think she ready."

Me: *"well, she is really good, in fact, she is my right-hand person, and our customers love her.*
Supervisor: Yes, but she is always so quiet in meetings and doesn't say much or add value in them – I am sure she does good work, but let's consider her next round.
Next round, that's in twelve months. The rule that was important to my supervisor was participation and contribution in meetings – she was doing great work, and her customers loved her. But those were her "rules". Do you know what are the rules for your organization, within your function or business group or

your senior management? If you don't know, then you can't do the next one effectively.

Create Green X's

Creating a green X is creating something memorable so that when you name some up, people remember something positive that you have recently done. The operative word here is: recently. If you were in our workshops, I would be drawing a short red line followed by two green X's, then another short red line and green X's to fill the top of a flipchart.

Create Green

X's

(SOMETHING MEMORABLE)

The red lines represent things that are not favorable or things you might have gotten wrong, and the green X's are the positive things that you have done that your senior management remembers. Because here is what happens when your name comes up, people are remembering either your red lines, or will they remember you more because of your memorable green X's.

Do they go, Brenda, wasn't she the one that leads that cross-functional team, yes, and wasn't she the one that asked that great question at the Town Hall, oh yes, yes, and wasn't she the one that was on the opening ceremony committee as well? We all like her; she is so active in our organization. I think she will go far.

It's not that we all don't have a few red lines, the question is do you have enough green X's that people will remember you? Your job is to create Green X's proactively.

CREATING A MEMORABLE GREEN X'S.

I was giving a talk titled «Winning in the Work World – How to Stand out in Your Organization» at one of the top 4 insurance companies in the USA. After my talk, one of the participant›s hand wrote a letter to me. Not only that, in that letter, but she also thanked me and paraphrased many of the insights I spoke about and presented them back to me. (that showed me she listened to me). She even reminded me and described where she was sitting in the auditorium because she asked a question during Q & A and wanted me to remember who she was.

How many people do you think would even think of handwriting a note? (In my case only one out of two hundred) and she used my words and gave it back to me in her content.

Now just let me explain something. When you take the same words, your senior leaders use and give it back to them – they think you are brilliant. I hope you caught that; I did not say use your words, I said to use their words. This lady was brilliant, and she knew how to be visible. Now I go around the world reading her letter out to make my point.

It would help if you found ways to create green X's so that when your name comes up, senior management has something positive to say about you. First and foremost, you need to understand the RULES of THE GAME, for that person, and before that, you need to DECIDE if you want to be seen as GREAT in the organization by senior management. Do not complain about someone else who is prepared to do what it takes if you are not.

Do you see how all these philosophies fit together? If you do, you are ready to start on your journey through the book with me.

Small Percent = Big Results

This book is about small adjustments and changes you can make that will significantly impact the way you connect, communicate, and stand out in an organization—or really anywhere. Are you aware of the things you need to do to make an impact and stand out; and if you are aware, how often do you actually do them? You can approach your career with one of four different mindsets. Take a look at the four mindsets in the **Behavioral Approach Pyramid** below. Put a check beside the level at which you see your attitude towards your current position (be honest). Do you know

Where do you see yourself?		Where do others see you?
☐	**WIN**	☐
☐	**CONTRIBUTE**	☐
☐	**CRUISE**	☐
☐	**SURVIVE**	☐

BEHAVIORAL APPROACH PYRAMID

Take a minute to honestly think through your approach in your current role and if there are other roles you play within or outside the organization that you rank differently. What could you be doing to have others rate you higher?

how others see you? Where do you think your supervisor or other co-workers might place you on the pyramid?

The bottom two mindsets, to **cruise** or merely to **survive**, are the ones that too many people naturally adopt, but the top two—contribute and win—are what it really takes to stand out. So, you first have to decide if you want to win, contribute, or just survive and cruise along in your job. If you decide you want to contribute or win, then you have to figure out how to get noticed and be re-membered.

That's where the 5% Zone comes into the picture. You may be wondering, "Why is it the 5% Zone and not the 80% Zone, or 100%, or some other number?" It's pretty simple. All I want you to focus on are the critical situations on the job—that 5% of the time—that you will have to "step up your game" if you want to get noticed, add value, be more energized, and help solve prob-lems. While it's true that some people naturally perform at higher percentages, 5% is the perfect place to start, and it's all you really need to outshine the competition.

This is good news! Why? I'm not asking you to make drastic 100% changes—because little changes can have big effects. As hu-man beings, we are creatures of habit, which means we are set in many of our behaviors and ways; however, I promise if you are will- ing to make some small changes that we will discuss in this book, the results will amaze you.

So as we get started, let me ask you these key questions:

1) Are you prepared to make a 5% change (not 100%, not even 50%—just 5%)

   ❑ Yes   ❑ No

2) Are there aspects of your work, interactions, and attitudes at work where you know you can make a 5% change to get better results?

❑ Yes   ❑ No

3) Are there some small things in your personal life that you could change to give you major benefits?

❑ Yes   ❑ No

If your answer to one or all three of these questions is "yes" (and for many of us, hopefully that's the obvious answer), then you're ready to stand out from the crowd. Once you "step up your game" into that 5% Zone, you will leave others wondering what you've got and why you are so good at what you do.

If your answer was "no," then what one, two or three small changes will you be willing to make to STAND OUT more and get further ahead in your career or business?

What Change Do I Need to Make?

Change 1) _____

What will I do: _____

_____

_____

_____

_____

_____

_____

_____

Change 2) _____

What will I do: _____

_____

_____

_____

_____

_____

_____

_____

_____

_____

Change 3) _____

What will I do: _____

_____

_____

_____

_____

_____

_____

_____

_____

_____

_____

ROMANS ARE LOOKING
FOR OTHER ROMANS

Here's the old adage:
All roads lead to... Rome.
In Rome do as the Romans... Do.

But outside of Rome...
Romans are looking for other Romans.

Here is what I mean. The leadership at corporate headquarters (Rome) is looking for other Romans (leaders) who look and feel and sound like them to lead their legions. If you work in another city or another country, and you do not sound like, look like, or act like the other "Romans," why would they allow you to lead their legions somewhere in their far flung empire? So, you need to understand what the Romans at your HQ look and sound like and what Rome wants out of its people. It's a global stage. Romans are looking for other Romans. Do you match up? Do you look like a Roman leader to your Rome (your HQ)? This is a critical distinction you have to recognize in global organizations. And remember that each company is slightly different—each company has its own needs, culture, goals, and expectations. So, find out what your own specific company looks for and make sure you are matching up.

What is GEM?

In order to understand exactly what the 5% Zone is and how it relates to your career in any facet of business or in any organization, it's important to understand the importance of adopting a Global Executive Mindset, or GEM. GEM is the basis of most of my training, and we will get into the aspects of GEM in more detail later in the book; but first I want to introduce the concept of GEM and its seven key facets. When you use you're 5% Zone philosophies along with the seven facets, you'll be on your way to standing out and making a difference.

Do you know the behavioral skill sets that are necessary to conduct business and play on a much larger scale? Do you know exactly how to communicate confidently, connect personally, and stand out in the corporate world? The GEM Behaviors will help you do just that.

Here are the behaviors that GEM fosters and promotes:

1. **Take Ownership**

   This includes showing initiative, suggesting new ideas, and willingly participating on teams.

2. **Build Trust**

   This behavior includes the ability to meet commitments, act with integrity, and influence at all levels within your organization.

3. **Communicate Confidently**

   Confident communication includes asking timely questions, interjecting proactively, and sharing your valid points of view.

4. **Provide Direct Feedback**

   This can include pushing back with appropriate assertiveness, sharing any negative views early, and providing sensitive feedback.

5. **Articulate Points of View Clearly**

   This behavior requires you to get to the point, communicate clearly, and display cultural sensitivity.

6. **Connect Personally**

   When you connect personally, you know how to connect with people, leverage formal and informal meetings, and develop relationships within all levels of your organization.

7. **Coach and Recognize Others**

   When you master this behavior, you can help others achieve their goals, guide and mentor others, and recognize and reward the efforts of others openly.

That could be an overwhelming list of attributes for some. Does adopting a GEM, a Global Executive Mindset, mean that you have to focus on all seven of these behaviors all the time? Absolutely not! And that's the best part. By focusing on a 5% change—or in other words, by choosing just 5% of the times in your career when you need to increase your performance or intensity—this means that you can focus on one or a few aspects of your GEM at a time. You simply have to take that extra step in 5% of the situations you face and put in the extra effort that will generate explosive results. Think about it this way. Imagine if you spent a few hours brain- storming for new ideas that will make an upcoming merger more successful for both companies involved. This may not even technically be in your "job description," but you know that it will be appreciated and get you noticed. Well, coming up with new ideas is just one small part of the "Take Ownership" facet of GEM; but that one act, that one time you step into the 5% Zone, could lead to a promotion or to your superiors finally sitting up and taking notice of you. It could set you apart.

It's not rocket science—it's small steps that lead to big changes. In fact, a 5% change in the way you act or think could lead to a 100% change in your life and career.

"SHE WAS ALWAYS A GO-GETTER"

I had a meeting with an ex-colleague, Jean, who wanted some career advice. After we greeted each other, she said, "You heard Susan made VP." Then, more importantly, she qualified the statement by saying, "Well, she was always a go-getter, wasn't she?"

Susan and Jean joined the organization at the same time as senior managers. Now six years later, one was a Director, and another was two more levels ahead of her at VP – what happened?

What I noticed already six years prior, Susan was already showing the behaviors of a "Go-Getter."

She was always wanting to help in projects, participated constructively at meetings, and volunteered to do things within the function that nobody else wanted to do. She very quickly got noticed even in her early days when we talked about future talent at succession planning meetings.

After the meeting, I was thinking to myself - Isn't this what most people should be doing (go-getting) if they want a career in an organization?"

How You Respond

With some simple math, it's easy to determine that if you focus your most conscious efforts in the 5% Zone, this means that 95% of your behaviors or activities are not up for discussion right now. Why is this? Why am I leaving 95% of your "normal behavior" alone? Well, this 95% represents the times in your life (which is most of the time) when your normal *modus operandi* is perfectly acceptable and will get you where you need to go. But it's that other 5% of the time and how you respond that will change your life.

In order to demonstrate how your 95% normal mode makes decisions and how you can make a conscious change into the 5% Zone, take a look at the Response Cycle diagram below:

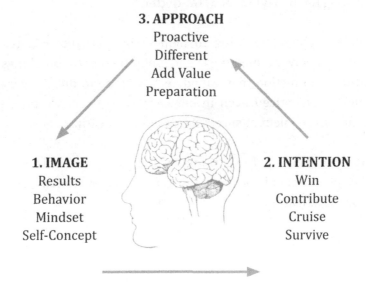

3. APPROACH
Proactive
Different
Add Value
Preparation

1. IMAGE
Results
Behavior
Mindset
Self-Concept

2. INTENTION
Win
Contribute
Cruise
Survive

THE RESPONSE CYCLE

Part One of the diagram represents the different aspects that have helped form and continue to form your self-image. **Part Two** lists the different mindsets with which you can approach any work or life situation (which are also the four parts of the Approach Pyramid from page 105). Once you choose your approach in Part Two, **Part Three** provides the choices you have for where to place your focus and how to approach those 5 situations with senior management, and this is where the 5% and your response cycle comes in.

In most situations, your focus can be as it usually is; in other words, you can make a decision according to what makes you feel the most comfortable or according to what you would normally do. But then you need to figure out the times—the 5% situations—where it would make a big difference for you to be more *proactive, think differently, add value,* or do some extra *preparation.* The trick—and it is a trick—is to convince yourself that you can do it when you are looking for excuses and justifications for why you can't.

There is an old saying that goes: *There's nothing new under the sun.* Well, the same goes for most of the things we see and hear. That's why we can hear something and immediately think: "This is a bunch of baloney" or "She's got a point" or "This idea has merit" or "This is totally opposite to my experience and I reject it" or "This is totally opposite to my experience, but since many other successful professionals have used it, I should at least consider it."

I'm not asking you to jump off a plane (but if you do, please use a parachute), pour your life savings into a business idea, or even be the next CEO of your organization (although why not— that certainly is a good goal). I'm not even asking you to turn over a new leaf and be someone you are not. I don't want to touch or change who you are—your 95%. I am only interested in your 5% moments.

And frankly, there are times in your life when all you really need to focus on are the most important 1% moments, as you will see from the following story about how a friend took full advantage of a 1% moment

SEIZING A 1% MOMENT

A friend of mine left for a promised future in country A, but he was cheated and swindled out of his life savings. He decided to pack up his bags and move to country B. With $300 in his pocket, he landed, checked into a hotel, and decided he needed to find some work by focusing on what he was good at right away to pay for his living expenses. He could have sulked, moaned, and writhed in self-pity for months. But he decided to move on—and do so quickly.

Six years later, I found myself sitting in his brand new 7 Series BMW with all the bells and whistles. In that one moment six years before, he could have laid down on his hotel bed and felt sorry for himself. But instead, he chose to act— to go against his Little Voice inside his head that told him he was too depressed to do anything—and that one small action made all the difference in his life.

It is going to take a little time and practice to become familiar with the response cycle mindset. You've programmed your mind your entire life to react in certain ways to specific stimuli, so retraining yourself to act differently in 5% of the situations will take some conscious effort. Take a good look at the table on the following page. The three rows—**How you Think, How you Operate, and How you Act**—are processes or actions we encounter countless times each day, often without even consciously thinking about them. And the three bullets below describe each of the columns in the table:

- *The 95% column* is what your brain instinctively tells you to do (notice the word "normal" appears in each reaction).

- *The 5% column* is what you have to train yourself to focus on when you need to be in your 5% Zone.

- *The Examples of 5% column* shows you some general ex- amples of what your 5% may look like. Notice that each of these activities or thoughts requires just that—*thinking* before acting! That's why the 5% Zone involves conscious effort to react in a way that is not like your 95% normal behavior.

	95%	5%	Examples of 5%
How You Think	Normal chat- ter and self- talk	Cued on focused, constructive self-talk	What an athlete says to himself before a race. An executive before presentation to the board. Before your presentation
How You Operate	Normal day-to-day activities	Important, key activities to achieve goals	Need to negotiate with new vendor on important project Preparing questions for CEO at all- hands meeting Your plan for big birthday surprise
How You Act	Normal self, need or want to be true to yourself Need to blend in or hide	Need to step up or standout in a specific situation or interaction Want to step up and help	Use set up statements to emphasize important point Push back Positively or Neutrally for your idea Volunteer to lead projects

In many situations in business (and in life) you have a choice to stand out, get your message heard, and become the leader you need to be at a specific moment. And in order to do that, you need to act from your 5% Zone. Here are some examples of situations where you can choose to stand out:

- Your boss needs someone to organize the benchmark visit by a high-profile external group.

- Your functional head from HQ is looking for someone to lead a companywide cross-functional project.

- The company is looking for someone to open up a new market that will take you away from home for up to two months.

These are just a few examples of times in your business life where you can choose to act from your 5% Zone. Begin to look for more opportunities, and you'll be amazed how many there actually are.

1. What situations / opportunities within your **TEAM** did you miss previously?

    _____

    _____

    _____

    _____

    What was your justification (excuse) for not doing them?

    _____

    _____

    _____

    _____

2. What situations / opportunities in your **FUNCTIONAL** group did you miss previously?

_____

_____

_____

_____

What was your justification (excuse) for not doing them?

_____

_____

_____

_____

3. What situations / opportunities in your **ORGANIZATION** did you miss previously?

_____

_____

_____

_____

What was your justification (excuse) for not doing them?

_____

_____

_____

_____

4. What **OTHER** situations / opportunities did you miss previously?

_____

_____

_____

_____

What was your justification (excuse) for not doing them?

_____

_____

_____

_____

CHOOSE TO BE DIFFERENT: ARDI'S STORY

It was time to present the final project for a yearlong HIPO program, and I had just coached the participants in the program on GEM and presentation skills. There were six countries represented: China, India, Australia, Malaysia, Singapore, and Indonesia. As you might expect, some of the participants were better at speaking English than others. Ardi, who was from Indonesia, did not speak the best English, and he felt he was going to get creamed by the others after he had seen them perform earlier that day. But instead of sulking and talking himself out of the game, he came up to me privately and said, "Stephen, I want to beat all of them. Can you help me?"

My response was YES—although I actually had some reservations. Then I added, "Are you sure?"

"Oh yes!" he replied emphatically.

He started to work through all the techniques we discussed in class and decided how he was going to be different and "stand out" to the regional management team. As I went on my rounds to visit each group and assess their progress, Ardi approached me again. "Stephen," he said, "I've got it! I'm going to start from the last slide [the financials/results] and go in reverse order through my presentation, and then end on my first slide." I helped him move a couple of slides to make the sequence work better, and then he was ready.

He was the fourth presentation, following powerhouses Australia, India and China's presentations. It was his turn; Ardi stood up and said, "Ladies and Gentlemen, I am going to start from my last slide.

You could almost hear everyone in the room go "damn!" in their heads. Then he went through his deck "backwards" and finally he said, "And this is why all of you should adopt this project in your country". All his colleagues stood up and gave him a standing ovation. (the only peer who got one.)
Ardi, the less-than-perfect English speaker, had just out-played, out- thought, and out-maneuvered the others because he truly wanted to WIN. I was really proud of this guy and the regional team was also greatly impressed. If Ardi can do it, then why can't you?

3 BLIND MICE

Recently a senior executive called me into his office to discuss providing the opportunity for his six direct reports to improve their communication skills to senior management. He only needed help for three but wanted to keep the opportunity fair and open to everyone.

He required specific help to improve their presentations and Q & A's skills with the senior team. He revealed to me on an excel chart a detailed report on their strengths, their opportunities, and areas he specifically wanted help for them.

This boss had done his homework, and he knew exactly the help they each needed. Here comes the kicker – he told everyone they had the option of getting coaching from an external consultant for their communication skills to senior management if they thought they needed it.

The irony of the situation, the three that were rank order the highest by the executive opted for the coaching, and **the three that needed it the most - declined** – how ironical.

Just two points, firstly, I notice this phenomenon all the time, the great ones want to get even better and the ones who think they are good

(and in this case, they were not, according to their boss) – find some excuse why they don't need it.

Secondly, if your supervisor suggests you get some development, take it – if you don't, it might just reflect poorly against you.

"The 5% Zone is comprised of points in time where you need to consciously *switch* to your most effective mode in order to come across with your best foot *forward.*"

— STEPHEN KREMPL

Part II

SO WHAT IS THE PROBLEM?

Your Little Voice

It all seems simple enough, right? Just react differently 5% of the time. It'd be great if all of the folks reading this saw the need for finding the 5% Zone in their careers. But perhaps you're thinking something like this right now instead:

> *"My colleagues will think I'm trying to suck up."*
>
> *"Why should I change? I am already good."*
>
> *"This is a bunch of hogwash."*
>
> *"I tried something like this before, and it doesn't work."*
>
> *"That other person tried it and got fired!"*

We all talk to ourselves all the time. We all have that little voice that goes with us everywhere and provides constant commentary during our everyday lives. If you think you don't you have that little voice, you might be saying this to yourself right now, *"What little voice? That's nonsense. I don't talk to myself."*

Well guess what? That just proves that you talk to yourself!

Your constant companion—your Little Voice—it can be useful. But it can also be a detriment. Have you ever thought about doing something great? I bet you have. You decide that it's finally time to speak up and share your point of view, introduce your new idea, or volunteer to be the lead person for the new project. But then your Little Voice took over and said something like this:

- *"Nah! I'm not that person. There are so many others who are better than me."*

- *"You don't need too; your work will speak for itself."*

- *"I can't. I am too new."*

- *"I don't have enough experience."*

- *"I'm not good enough."*

- *"Maybe next time. I am too busy right now."*

- *"You don't understand. My situation is different."*

- *"I don't have the right background."*

- *"My upbringing... my grandma told me... my uncle said... my best friend pointed out..."*

- *"Oh, but my colleagues and my boss are terrible."*

- *"I can't believe my luck—I have such lousy team."*

If you allow your Little Voice to run the show, you will never be short on justifications for why you *can't* do something. So, it's time to start recognizing which of these excuses or justifications you use to make you feel most comfortable.

Most of us have a "default" excuse—our go-to justification for why we won't or can't do something. Here is a simple exercise. In the following box, write down your favorite excuse for why you won't do something that you know is important for you to accomplish:

MY FAVORITE EXCUSES ARE:

1) _____

2) _____

3) _____

My #1 favorite excuse is:

_____

_____

_____

I remember recently using it for this situation:

_____

_____

_____

If you never step out of your *Comfort Zone*
and into the *5% Zone*, you will not
get to where you want to be in
your business or life.

I've heard many "favorite" excuses over the years, and, every culture and country has their own kinds of excuses. Here's an example: "Well Stephen, in China, we don't like to stand out, and we are humble and not so outspoken. We have been brought up that way." To this I can say that I know plenty of Asians who are not that way; and if you want to leave an impression, you better be doing some - thing different than your normal 95% self tells you to do.

If you are a quiet, introverted type (which I myself am), then speaking up or asking questions in a group might be tough for you—but that's exactly why you need to switch to you 5% zone to overcome this part of your behavior. Just because you feel more comfortable behaving in a certain way doesn't mean that you should keep doing it all the time. Let me put it this way:

BRENDA'S OLD SCRIPT

Brenda was a shy Asian who was attending one of my workshops. An hour into my presentation, she spoke up (in a whiny tone): "Ah Stephen, you don't understand. We are Asians, and we are not like that. We cannot do these things that you are telling us."

Fast forward to the next afternoon, and Brenda is the most animated, vibrant person in the group now asking (in a deep confident voice): "Stephen, how do I get more opportunities to get in front of groups in my company?

So what happened to Brenda? I focused her on finding her own 5%. Once she knew she did not have to do it all the time—none of us do—she realized she could step outside her comfort zone for 5% of the time and create huge results. You can come around that quickly as well. You just need the right constructive guidance. As Tony Robbins, **entrepreneur, #1 NY Times best-selling author, philanthropist, and the nation's #1 life and business strategist** says: **"Knowledge is Potential, Action is Power. "** Most people are missing out because they have not practiced and put into action the behavioral skills found in GEM to ensure their chances of getting ahead are exponentially higher.

In a book that I highly recommend called *Little Voice Mastery* by Blair Singer, he writes that in order to stop your Little Voice (which Singer calls your "LV") you have to start talking back to it! The next time your LV hands you your default excuse for why you aren't the best person for the job or why your skill set just doesn't compare to the competition, you must say something to your LV like:

"Thank you, that's a nice story, but now let's get on with it!"

You must tell your LV something that will allow you to counter act the negative excuse that your LV is trying to make into your reality. Look at it this way: You are already talking to yourself, so you might as well choose something to say that is more useful!

If you're thinking right now, *"That's a stupid idea,"* you must realize that this is your LV talking, but your LV doesn't have to be the one to dictate your thoughts or actions anymore. I'm not saying there is one cut-and-dry way to mentally react when you hear a new idea; I'm simply alerting you to your mind's messages—especially if you need to perform at a higher level right away in front of an important group or person.

But many of us have such an overbearing feeling that we can't do it; we're not good enough; or we need more information, more training, or more coaching before acting. That's how we paralyze ourselves and then justify why it is so. We all do it—some of us just do it less often and choose to focus on more positive things in order to switch into our 5% Zones when needed.

You must become more aware of your normal "self-talk," those back and forth conversations you have with your LV. And remember that it all comes back to that number, that 5%. It is in the 5% Zone that your courage, your spirit to win, your ability to add value, and ultimately your confidence lies. If you can learn to switch from your 95% normal behavior to the 5% bigger, better you, then this will be the key to unlocking that big break, that big promotion, or that big change you want.

To make it easier to control your LV, I also created the **GEM Self-Talk Model** to help you better decipher the inner dialogue that—until now—has kept you performing in your normal, predictable ways, thus ignoring the need for the 95%/5% split. Take a look at the model below and on the next page. We all experience steps 1 through 3 on a regular, even daily, basis.

Here is how it works inside our heads:

GEM SELF-TALK MODEL

STEP 1

An issue or situation arises at work or in life
You start to think about it (and talk about it to yourself)

STEP 2

You begin looking for the "correct" response
in one of two ways:

By searching previous experience and giving your
predetermined response

OR

You have an open mind about the outcome (Whichever option
makes you feel comfortable, safe, or allows you to be in control)

STEP 3

You respond in one of two ways: Your normal 95% way

OR

Your 5% way

Now that you understand how self-talk works inside your head, take a look at the diagram on the next page for a graphical representation of the GEM Self-Talk Model. As you can see, when an **"Issue"** arises (which can be something minor like an email from a customer to a solo presentation you are planning to give to upper management), one of two voices in your head speaks up— either your **"Constructive LV or LV1"** (LV stands for little voice) or your **"Detrimental LV or LV2."** Choosing to listen to your LV 1 leads you to have a more open mind and will help you find your **"5% Zone,"** whereas choosing to listen only to your LV 2 forces your brain to lean only on past experience, thus missing a chance to shine as you retreat to your **"Regular Thinking Zone"** (aka your normal 95% mode). It's up to you to choose to listen to your constructive LV 1.

It is said that we only use about 3 to 8% of our mental capacity (often called the conscious mind), and the remaining 92% is comprised of our subconscious, which is our "autopilot" that runs our bodies—and where we spend resources talking to ourselves. It's no wonder why people can sit in a room in total silence

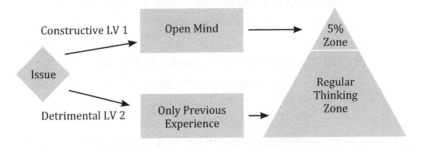

GLOBAL EXECUTIVE MINDSET
(GEM) SELF TALK MODEL

while the expressions on everyone's faces cover every possible range of human emotion. Our subconscious minds are constantly reacting to everything we see, hear, touch, taste, and feel— sometimes whether we want it to or not!

Here are a few examples to demonstrate what I mean:

- Think of your new baby at home—a **SMILE** naturally appears on your face.

- Think of a recent argument with a colleague—you most likely **FROWN**.

- Think of all the things you need to do after the meeting— you have that **ANXIOUS** look.

- Think about what to do for lunch—maybe you have a **BLANK** dream-like look.

- Think about the fact that you are up next to present—you might look **WIDE-EYED** and a little nervous (some people could show excitement, it just depends.)

When your subconscious reacts to a stimulus or something it hears, and then you react, how do you think you came to that conclusion? You compared it to some previous experience in your head—whether true or imagined—and "told" yourself how to react. You need to control these emotions and the expressions on your face, as most people can "read" expressions and sense if you are nervous, confident, or just plain bothered about something. Avoid such transparency, especially in the 5% of situations that matter most to you. This means you have to catch what you are saying to yourself that causes these nonverbal signals.

What do I typically say to myself when I face the following situations?

a) A boring presentation on a Video Conference Call (e.g. "What a waste of time.")

_____

_____

_____

_____

_____

_____

b) An idea brought up by someone else with which you disagree (e.g. "This idea is stupid. ")

_____

_____

_____

_____

_____

_____

c) When someone beat you to articulating a point that you were just thinking about bringing up (e.g. "What a show-off.")

_____

_____

_____

_____

_____

Be careful what you say to yourself in these or other situations at work, as it may distract you from focusing on how or what you need to do next to stand out versus simply getting annoyed, angry, or even jealous.

Here is a tough situation that could arise at work:

Your peer just told a visiting SVP from HQ why her "pet" project was delayed and insinuated that you were the cause of it because you were not supportive since you did not come up with the idea. In reality, it was your idea and you were supportive, but it was delayed because of the customer's request. You now have to do damage control:

What do you say to yourself? How do you react?

1) I am going to confront that @#! colleague!

2) Rehearse in your head how you are going to defend yourself to the SVP.

3) Scheme of ways to get back at your colleague.

4) Let it go and focus on getting the job done.

Your choice may give you a clue to the way you react in similar situations. Maybe you responded the way you did because of thoughts like, "I can't stand those types of people" or "I've been burned like that before" or "I should have approached the SVP first" or "I am really not good at this politics stuff."

So, ask yourself, what did you say in your head to make you choose that response?

_____

_____

_____

_____

I hope you recognize now why you need to take control of your LV 2 in your 5% situations; otherwise, some of you may talk yourself out of seizing the opportunity to become more Visible.

MY LV AH-HAH

A county manager wrote me an email after our program and said, "You know, after a few days of reflection – I realized my real problem is my LV2, and I am determined to address it.

Now at least I will stay vigilant and block it out as hard as I can, especially when those 5% opportunities arise with my executive committee members.

Why Most of Us Don't Change

Many of us have the best of intentions to make change happen, whether it is to exercise more, read more books, be more social, take more study courses, or just stand out more. So why do so many of us talk ourselves out of such positive change? In addition to your Little Voice, there are several key reasons why you won't change (or more to the point, don't think you can). See how many of the reasons listed below sound familiar:

- You've adopted a sense of complacency.
- You blame the bad economy.
- Your friends have discouraged you.
- You get little or no spouse/partner support.
- Someone else already had the idea before you.
- You simply don't think you can.
- It's just not the "right time."
- You don't have all the information you need to act.
- You don't have enough money.

What other reasons can you come up with for your own life and situations? Most of us have quite a few. Take a minute and list a few of them on the following lines:

Reasons I don't like to change:
(And if you have not written anything up to this point in the book reveals a 95% tendency you may have.)

_____

_____

_____

_____

_____

_____

_____

My **default** excuse for not wanting to change is (I'm sure it is a logical and legitimate excuse for 95% of the times—just don't use it 100%. And if you recognize it, you will be fine):

_____

_____

_____

_____

_____

_____

_____

Because of the reasons listed above (and maybe even a lot more you didn't list), you are not ready to make a *dramatic* change in your life or career. That's okay. In fact, that's great—because I'm just asking you to make a 5% change.

YOU DON'T HAVE TO BE THE FIRST

Motorola invented the cell phone and its related technologies. They were the first—and they dominated the market in the early days. The question is: Where are they now? Where was Samsung, LG, or Apple in those early days? Nowhere! So even if you are "late to the party" in adopting Global Executive Mindset skill sets, it doesn't mean you can't catch up. Decide now that you can be better than anybody you take on. You have a very good chance if you leverage your 5% zone.

In my seminars and workshops, I have my audience select one or two of their reasons and do an exercise that I call the Focus Ring. With this technique, you pick one of your reasons and then begin figuring out how to eliminate it from this list of excuses holding you back.

During the Focus Ring exercise, you focus on what you can control and then focus on techniques that will help you overcome this reason like being more prepared, becoming proactive rather than reactive, and searching for ways to add value to situations (the options from Step 3 of the Your Response Cycle). In my workshops and especially during this exercise, I always remind participants that when you don't feel like speaking up is exactly the time you *should* be speaking up. Use a positive statement—or the opposite of your excuse—to motivate yourself.

Now create that statement that is opposite of your excuse and use it when your 5% opportunities appear:

_____

_____

_____

_____

_____

BRITTANY'S STORY—WHAT'S YOUR EXCUSE?

The following is an actual interaction that took place in my workshop. One participant in particular simply had no idea how she came across. We had just talked about energy levels prior to this exchange, and we were answering the question: *What is your excuse?* Here is how the interaction went:

Stephen: So, let's hear from somebody from Table 1 who has not spoken before. Please share at least one excuse for why you can't volunteer for the new project or contribute more at work. Alright?

Brittany: My excuse is, I don't have time [spoken fairly quietly level 4 out of 10].

Stephen: You are too soft and it's nowhere close to 7 volume level.

Brittany: I don't have time [said slightly louder].

Stephen: Try again. That was 5, I need 7 Come on.

Brittany: I don't have time [not much louder].

Stephen: Okay, that's a 6. You're working up, not bad. Try again.

Brittany: I don't have time [barely louder].

Stephen: That was a 6.2. 7 is the minimum level, my dear. You're holding back a lot.
Why are you holding back? What's your name?

Brittany: Brittany. I feel I am shouting.

Stephen: Does anybody in the room think Brittany is shouting?

Audience: [Everyone shaking their heads and saying NO]

Stephen: Now, Brittany, can you shout for me.

Brittany: I don't have time [spoken a little louder].

Stephen: That was 6.8. Wait! Let's pretend I'm Dr. Phil. "I'm sitting right here, Brittany, and I can tell you that you are not a loud person even when you think you are. Who told you, 'You should not be a loud person.'"?

Brittany: Myself.

Stephen: See that? It eventually came out. That's what I'm telling you. Unless you get to that, you're not going to solve the problem. It's okay, Brittany. It's the little voice that tells you why you can't speak up. You gave me your favorite excuse, but you couldn't even say it loud enough for the whole room to hear. So, I got you from a 4 to a 6.8, which is not bad. Do you think you can now be a loud person? I give you permission to be a loud person. Okay? I blessed you and you are now a loud person. So, give me a 7 or higher

Brittany: I don't have time [spoken at 7.5 level].

Stephen: Now that's a 7. All right, much better. Give her a round of applause to Brittney

Unless you are frank with yourself, you can easily justify why you are the way you are 100% of the time for reasons that may not be useful all the time. Remember you need the GEM behaviors 5% of the time. You can do that—even Brittany did!

Most individuals don't even know how loud or soft they are in meetings, and if you are remote and not even in the same room, it might be worse. I have heard people mumble, swallow their words, or are just too soft. How do you think that comes across to senior management? Most of you don't even think about this. Remember, there is 95% meeting volume (a 5) and a 5% meeting volume (7 or little louder than your usual) - you must know the difference.

One Tough Question

Before we can get into the specifics of how you can stand out and how to utilize the 5% Zone through the use of some specific techniques, it's time to ask yourself one more question. It's a tough one, so are you ready? Here goes:

How do I come across to other people?

I am not only talking about how you come across to others within your team, but also to your entire functional group, to your colleagues from other divisions or business units, and even to business people from other countries. How do you come across to senior management? Are you the one they have labeled with "Leadership Potential?" Do they talk about you with words like: *Bright, Articulate, Insightful, Thorough,* or *Funny*?

And how about senior management from other countries? When you attend global or regional meetings, do they refer to you with phrases like: *Not Confident, Sticks to Himself, Doesn't Say Much,* or *Not Impressive*?

If you are part of a visiting business delegation representing your country, what would the foreign business owners or government officials say when you leave? What would anyone say when you leave a meeting or situation?

It's not what they say when you are in the room or leave the call, that is usually positive and corporate nice. It is what they say when you leave the meeting. Sometimes it goes like this:

Leader: "That was an excellent presentation Jim on the Agility idea – we need more ideas and people like you in the organization."

Jim: Smiles, says, "Thank You" and leaves the room

(or video conference call) pleased with himself.

Leader: Turning to the other senior team members. "That was confusing – were you clear about what he was talking about?"

I am not suggesting this happens in your organization, the question is, do you know what they are saying about your presentation or idea?

There's not a single one of us who wants to believe that others think of us in a "less than ideal" way. When it comes to our daily interactions with other human beings, our way of presenting ourselves just comes naturally to us (a combination of personallty and years of programmed responses), so we don't really even think about it. It's just *how we are*, so why worry about it, right? Well, not exactly. There are four important things you actually need to recognize about yourself:

1. Your Presence

It's important to understand your *presence*—how you come across to others. Most of us don't know how we come across unless we are actually videotaped during a presentation or program. And that's just one example of your presence.

How about the daily stuff like how your voice and tone sound when you introduce yourself to someone? How about your energy level, is it high or low? Do you know the difference when you are in person versus on call? Are your messages to the point or long-winded? Do you come across as confident or nervous? Leaders can tell even if they can't see you in person. How do you come across when you share a differing point of view or when you skillfully push back at a meeting - do you tend to be more positive or negative?

These are all crucial factors in how you are perceived, and they can make a massive difference in the influence you're able to have over others.

Your Ability to Connect

This is a tough one to gauge. You need to assess your ability to en- gage others whether you're in an entry-level position or managing other people. What is your skill at connecting with others at all levels within your organization? Can you connect in person versus a phone or video call? Many of us have blind spots and inadvertently treat individuals or groups at various levels differently. If you are disingenuous, people will know—so you need to start becoming more aware of this.

There is no limit to the number of people (from any and every level) with which you should connect. This includes people who manage the front desk, security guards, peers in your department, peers in other departments, supervisors, and even your supervisors' peers from other departments. How about senior management? Do they know you? If so, what would they say about you? If you want to stand out, you need to care. You are not running a political office—but in a sense you are. People like people they like.

Let me ask you another question: How do you judge others, their presence, and their ability to connect to you? What do you like or dislike about the way others attempt to connect? The point here is that there are likely some GEM behaviors that others do well that you perhaps do not do as well, and you therefore un- knowingly shy away from them because you don't like (or are not good at) that behavior.

I like how other people/colleagues come across when they:

1) _____

2) _____

3) _____

4) _____

5) _____

Things I dislike:

1) _____

2) _____

3) _____

4) _____

5) _____

Things I may be inadvertently shying away from because I dislike them in others (e.g. Asking Pertinent Questions. You may say to yourself, "When Tom asks questions, he is trying to show off." You don't want to appear as a "show off" so you don't ask questions—even though it might be a 5% meeting.):

1) _____

2) _____

3) _____

4) _____

5) _____

Things I need to get better at to make a better or bigger impression (by my communication style, my ability to connect, and how I plan to stand out):

1) _____

2) _____

3) _____

4) _____

5) _____

PAYING ATTENTION OR DOING EMAIL?

I am on a Video conference call, and I can see everyone, but sometimes people forget because they are by themselves in another location that I can see if you are paying attention or not. I can see all your expressions on your face, body language, and sometimes just for fun, I pick on those who are "not paying attention."

If it's an audio call, it's slightly different, but imagine you are running the conference call, then you ask "Stephen, what do you think about the point Sally has just made?" And Stephen goes, "Arrr, can you repeat the question?"

Do you think Stephen was paying attention or not paying attention? You guessed it, he probably had the phone on mute and was doing his email(now I know you don't do this) but do you know people who do this, and you try to save the day by asking to repeat the question. How do you think you will come across? Don't try this in your 5% calls.

2. How Often You Take Charge

For some of us, taking charge is just not in our DNA. Many of us are shy or lack the courage to take on the hard tasks, often because of discouragement from our Little Voice. For others, it probably happens far too often. Take a step back and look at how many times you've "stepped up to the plate." Is it too much? Not enough?

Organizations and leaders are looking for other leaders, who step in and take charge of things. No matter your personality or your natural tendencies, you need to find the right opportunities to take charge in a positive and helpful manner—and in a manner that will get you noticed in a good way.

If I went to your bosses' boss and asked them about you – what could they recently point to that you have taken charge of?

Imagine you have a task or a project that you want to assign to someone. Wouldn't you be glad if someone spoke up and said, "I am interested in leading that for you?" The same is true for other people's projects. Many times, in our training sessions or even in actual meetings, I have witnessed people passing the buck onto someone else to be the leader. It's not wrong to do that from time to time. What's wrong is when you let that opportunity slip past you every time.

Don't let your LV 2 talk you out of stepping up because of your favorite excuse (Which was what? Yep, you remember it well.). You need to forget that excuse and go after that 5% project, task or you need to lead to gain that visibility. And even if you don't get picked (which is unlikely after you put your hand up... because nobody else will), people will remember your willingness to step in and help (just like you remember a friend offering to help you move or help you on a project).

So here are some questions for you:

a) When was the last time you stepped up to take charge of something? Why did you step up? And if you haven't— why not?

_____

_____

_____

_____

b) Which project or task should you be preparing to   volunteer to lead that is coming up in the near future?

_____

_____

_____

_____

c) What should you be doing to **prepare, add value** and be **different** so that you will get picked?

_____

_____

_____

_____

3. Your Tendency to Help Others

Do you help others shine or learn? If you don't do this already, I'm here to tell you that other people have noticed. We all know "those people" who are only in it for themselves. So, your new mantra needs to be: *Whom can I help today?* It's amazing the gratification that will come from helping others. Take the time to help others, lend a hand on a project, provide ideas, or even give a word of encouragement in the hallway. If your supervisor has a problem he is dealing with, see if you can help—that will always get noticed.

Now I want to make a distinction between helping and giving people more work. In my GEM program for college students, we do an exercise where I go through a presentation and have people share their input on how to make it better. By the third slide, one of two things happens:

1.) People are too slow in offering help or

2.) They offer their "help" in the form of comments like, "Stephen, I think you should change that slide to make it look better or drop in a relevant video."

I quickly remind them they have just given me MORE WORK versus contributing more helpful comments like, "Stephen, I can easily animate that slide for you" or "I think I know where to find a couple of videos for you to look at." Now they are starting to help rather than assigning me additional work. Do you recognize the difference?

Have I been giving others (supervisors, colleagues) more work, or have I really been adding value? How can I add more value to the following people?

Bosses Boss

Supervisors

_____

_____

_____

Peers

_____

_____

_____

Staff

_____

_____

_____

Customers

_____

_____

_____

Other

_____

_____

_____

Remember if you are helping, then help! You may want to teach someone a technique or a short cut you have learned from your experience, but you first have to consider whether this person has the time at that moment to learn a new trick. It is your call—every situation is different. Just be aware of the outcome.

I remember a time when I was attempting to sell our services to a large customer. It represented a big consulting project. We went back and forth on details, content, timelines, meetings, and more meetings. I began to sense the process was stalling. I decided to try something "more practical," so I asked the client, "What does your CEO really want from this project?" The answer was so simple. All he wanted was to meet our CEO in person. He had seen videos, heard stories, but he wanted to actually meet our CEO face-to-face. I replied, "You've got to be kidding me. You should have told me that six months ago." After the two CEOs met, they signed the con- tract immediately. We landed the project because I stopped and took the time to find out how I could help them instead of focusing on my own desire, which was to get the contract signed. In the end, it was such a small and easy request. A small adjustment in strategy can equal a big payoff. *What can you do to get bigger results?*

These four points are so critical to you fitting in and succeeding across organizational situations, cultures, and levels. The real movers and shakers are more self-aware than ever before. This is the global game that is being played today, so you better be ready.

Are You Mining For Gold or Excuses?

By now you may at least be open to making small changes or adjustments so that you can have dramatic results. After all, small changes can lead to big improvements. When you fine tune your PC, slightly adjust a musical instrument, or tweak your car's engine, you improve the overall performance of each, right? Yes, those small changes are what it takes to achieve the great sound or performance that you need.

Did you know that top athletes focus on the smallest parts of their game—fine tuning critical movements or developing incremental mental strength—in order to gain much bigger results? The problem is that many of us say, "I have to radically change to get the results." (And yes, in certain situations a big change may be necessary.) But guess what? Even the big changes start with small steps. I'm sure you've heard the famous adage from Confucius:

> ## "The journey of a thousand miles begins with a single step."

I suppose a few lucky ones are able to enact change or turn over a new leaf overnight; and if you are a part of the "Overnight Success" group, then I suggest that you give this book away to someone who needs it. But how many people do you know who have turned their lives around in one day? No, most of us have to journey the entire thousand miles to get to where we want to be.

While there may not be very many in the "Overnight Success" group, I'm sure we all know quite a few people in another group. It's a group made up of people who won't change no matter what you tell them. People in this group have conceived the perfect story or experiences to justify why it cannot be done. Their sob stories usually begin with a line like this one (and you know we've all heard it before):

"But you don't understand. My situation is different..."
We used to meet face to face now we can't...

To these people I say this: We all have different situations. After all, we are all different! However, there are also many things in your situation that are similar to the situations of countless others before you.

So, what's the problem? These people are simply not willing to do what it takes to overcome their Little Voices and fight back. They choose to carry on with their lives in the same way they al- ways have and blame everyone else when they run into the same problems over and over again. They may be GOOD but they haven't decided to be GREAT and some think they already are.

We've all known people like this— or have thought this way ourselves from time to time. The natural tendency in human nature is to blame others for our inability to get things done in our lives. But that's just it—it's a tendency, not an ultimatum, which means you can fight it!

If you know someone in the "An Excuse for Everything" group, this book may not be for them either, unless you're prepared to show them how it all works or attend an event with them that al- lows them to experience success firsthand. Even if you gave this group of excuse makers a real gold coin, they'd claim it was a fake and try to prove that it's not worth anything.

So the question is, are you willing to accept the gold coin as real or just make more excuses? I can give you the gold coin; but I also want to show you how to mine for your own gold so that you have a continual source of gold coins for yourself. You will find that gold mine hidden somewhere in the 5% Zone. So, here's to you, the brave souls who are open to finding the vein of gold and learning how to "mine" your 5% difference.

Let me leave you with a thought, how do you know if you are good or great?

Sounds rhetorical, but the answer is simple: you are only as good or great as the person who comes before you or after you.

As an example, you may think you are a great presenter, but if the person who presents after you is better than you, then maybe you're not that great after all on that call.

In every corporation, there are lots of people eyeing for that promotion, high profile project, or recognition that you are seeking. Many of them prepare a little more and are a little more visible and have the business results to back them up.

If you want to WIN and be VISIBLE, then you have to ensure that you stay ahead of them, and we will show you how.

CONFERENCE CALL - 5% MOMENT

I just had my 5% moment with my vice president, Michelle (3 levels up), in a global manager's teleconference.

Used (almost) every technique you taught, suppressed my little voice, and asked a question. I took notes from the start, told myself, "game on!" asked my question, and created a green X.

I just wanted to say thanks for the training. If not for it, I would have logged on, listened, and logged off - my first time participating in a 5% meeting.

In the countless training I've had, this has been the one that has given me the most adrenalin and benefits applying.

"Successful people do what unsuccessful people are not willing to do."

— JEFF OLSON

Part III

THE 5% ZONE AND GEM

The GEM Differentiator

I hear the same things from them over and over again from executives. They all want their people to step up, take some ownership, be proactive and share their points of view. However, for many of the reasons we have already discussed, most people talk themselves out of making standout moves. But whether or not you work for a large multinational corporation, these skill sets are universally sought for, so it's time to figure out what you're doing and how to change.

The reality of the workplace is this: After you get your first job, nobody looks at your diploma or cares about what school you at- tended. I am not saying that higher education is not important; in fact, many times, the right school or degree is what gets your foot in the door in the first place. However, it is the way you express your thoughts, how you interact with various levels of the organization, your ability to gain people's trust, and how you get along with others that speaks much more loudly than your alma mater ever could.

We know that managers, executives, and CEOs everywhere are looking for special qualities in their employees, so how do we get there? It all comes back to the 7 Facets that I introduced in Part II called the Global Executive Mindset (GEM) behaviors.

Take a look at the diagram on the next page called the **GEM Model.** Each of the 7 Facets of GEM (found on the outside of the figure) are part of what helps make up the central, focal point of the diagram, which is your ability to STAND OUT.

THE GEM MODEL

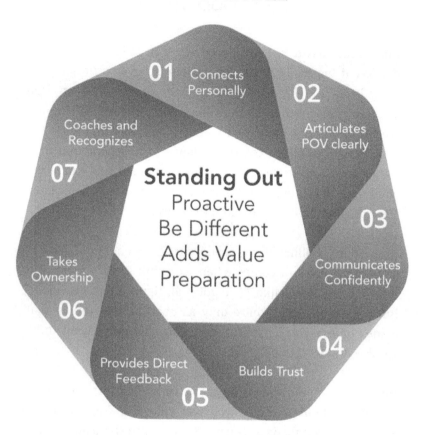

ARE YOU GOOD OR GREAT?

Jim Collins wrote a book called *Good to Great* in which he discussed his study of fifteen companies over a fifteen-year period. All of these companies had double-digit or high single-digit growth over the fifteen-year period. During the study, something happened to each company and then the results went through the roof. They were all *good* and then they became *great*. So, what really happened that made the companies go from good to great? Anybody? It was a decision. They decided that they wanted to be great.

In the book, Collins warns readers that the enemy of great is good. The problem comes when we think we are good, and then we say things like, "I've got it all figured out. I'm good." But remember that you're only as good as the person that comes before you or comes after you. You don't want to be good—you want to be great.

How many of you want to be great? Don't just settle for good. If you can figure how to best use your 5% Zone, you will accomplish exactly what you need in order to stand out in your corporation and be great. But you need to make that decision first. There are no right or wrong answers; it's just a choice.

Now that we know what the 7 facets are and that they play the critical role in standing out (and thus finding your 5% Zone), let's get into each of the facets in a little more detail:

Facet #1
Articulates Point of View (POV) Clearly

When you are asked to share your point of view in a meeting, how do you do it? What is the best way to share your POV that makes the most impact? And even more importantly, how do you frame your statement up front to guide your answer and keep your audience engaged? At my workshops, I call these your **SETUP STATE-MENTS**. Setup statements are statements that attract people's attention to your point and give you the framework to respond effectively! Here are some examples of good setup statements:

- "I have one point to make (or 2 points or 3 points)..."
- There are 3 strategic imperatives that I would.....
- "I would like to highlight a key idea..."
- "The most important point all of you have missed is..."

Making setup statements is easy when you practice thinking and responding with them, especially if you pay attention to what the person before you is saying rather than rehearse what you are going to say in your head as he or she is speaking.

As you make your point, it's also important to *get to the point!* No one likes it when you hem-haw around the issue. Make your statement in a concise and direct manner while focusing on communicating your point in a way that all levels can understand.

Why is this facet important? Your ability to articulate your POV is one of the most obvious ways others can tell that you think clearly, have an opinion, add value to a discussion, and come across as the confident leader they need. This skill is required in all the five situations, whether you are in person or remote.

Your polish and ability to act appropriately in these different situations in multiple international settings will put you in a small percentage of great leaders. Shoot for great!

In addition to getting to your point and being able to communicate appropriately at all levels, you also need to be able to show cultural sensitivity, especially in dealings across the globe. Your style will not necessarily change, but your first few minutes or the beginning of the interaction may have to change slightly. You have to **find out**, **adjust to,** and **respect** how things are done in that country. For example, in many countries, acknowledging the most senior person in the room is appropriate. In fact, in some countries, his exact title and salutations need to be stated first (and correctly!) before you can continue. You have to know these things, which means that you either need to ask something or pay special attention to what is going on around you.

How **GOOD** am I at this facet?

_____

_____

_____

_____

_____

What more do I need to do to be **GREAT** at this facet?

_____

_____

_____

_____

_____

PAY ATTENTION!

Many years ago, I was in Malaysia accompanying a senior leader off site to a two-day conference. On the first day after tea break, a "notable" training house (the first from the USA) was rolling out their latest material and their founder's new book, and a trainer from the company was up on stage going through his spiel. Halfway through the session, their CEO walked into the room (he was a Tan Sri, which is a title given to only a handful of individuals in the country), so he was important enough that everyone acknowledged him any time he entered a room. However, this particular trainer calmly proceeded with his presentation without acknowledging the CEO. The CEO walked to the middle of the large room, turned around, and walked straight out, as protocol was not followed. The host and others were scrambling to fix the situation and called an emergency tea break.

Now we can argue that the trainer did not know this rule of procedure. However, if he had paid attention to all that happened that morning and took the time to learn the way business was conducted, all he had to do was stop for two seconds and nod, acknowledge the CEO's name, and then carry on. Instead, he committed a minor (or major depending on how you look at it) international faux pas.

Pay attention and focus on what's going on around you, not only on your message. This applies as much to a minor meeting as it does to a major presentation like the one in this story. We simply spend too much time focusing on our own message.

Facet #2
Communicates Confidently

When you speak up, remember everyone in the room or on the call is consciously and unconsciously comparing you against everyone else. So how do you distinguish yourself and stand out by communicating effectively and confidently? You need to be able to do three things:

1) Share your Point Of View (POV) clearly.

2) You must also be able to share your Point Of Concern (POC). It's important to help others understand why you may not agree with what's being said.

3) You must also use Third Party Validation (TPV) in a way that supports the points that you are sharing. One way of sharing your POC by using a validating statement like: "The data from our customers research shows these 3 key opportunities ..."

You also need to be able to ask timely, impactful questions, know how to interject proactively, and be prepared to share your POV and POC and use TPV. To share your POV, thank the person who went immediately before you for making their point, and then add your point of view like this: "Stephen, Zoe makes a great point. My point of view is..." To share your POC, you can use a statement like: "I have a different point of view" or "My idea is slightly different." Any time you have a differing opinion from someone else, it's important to understand that it's okay to let others know. So, when you encounter someone with whom you have a difference of opinion, simply **Interject**, **Thank** the person, and then **Respond**. It doesn't mean you have to agree with everything, and there may be many times when you do not agree, but you can choose to respond with both professionalism and confidence.

Why is this facet important? I have a different take on this than most people. Most would say that it is only common courtesy to share your concerns or your POV with professionalism. And yes, that is true; but the real key is that it is not only what happens IN the meeting or discussion that counts, but also what people are going to say or remember about you AFTER you leave. You want people to say something like, "Jill really added value here, and I liked her perspective" instead of "Steve was just being a jerk."

Remember, this is not what needs to happen at every single meeting. It would be nice if it did, but that's probably not realistic. These are your 5% meetings with key individuals in the organization or external parties who are on your 5% list with whom you need to have your best foot forward.

How **GOOD** am I at this facet?

_____

_____

_____

_____

_____

_____

_____

What more do I need to do to be **GREAT** at this facet?

_____

_____

_____

_____

_____

_____

_____

Facet #3
Connects Personally

One of the key skills that distinguish people with leadership potential from the rest of the crowd is your ability to interact and have conversations with people at different levels of your business or organization. This includes the ability to show interest and give enough information about your own self to be interesting to others. Most people who attend my programs or use the online program seem to have no problem dealing with peers who are on their same level or with those who are below them. They seem to run into problems, how- ever, when they deal with bosses or supervisors in both formal and informal situations.

If this sounds like you, then your focus should be on developing relationships at all levels within your organization, which means you need to learn how to leverage both formal and informal meetings (i.e. small chat at the start of calls, lunches, time on the elevator, unplanned encounters).

Why is this facet important? Knowing how to connect with people, leverage formal and informal meetings, and develop relationships at all levels is key to moving up in an organization. How many of you realize that the ability to develop relationships at all levels (not just at your peer level) is an important attribute? The question is how good are you compared to your local and foreign peers? Learn to overcome the LV issues that commonly surface when communicating with higher levels, which might sound like: "I feel a little uncomfortable" or "I don't know what to say" or "I don't know what to ask."

The ability to talk and have a conversation is the art of asking the right questions and paying attention to their responses. We suggest you use the acronym FORMING. FORM will allow you to express interest in the person, and ING is having something interesting about yourself when the person turns to you, and they say, "what are you interested in?" You should be able to launch straight into that story.

So, your real task is to find out what category or topic they (senior management) are most interested in and then let them talk. If you learn this critical skill, you will be able to talk to anybody about anything.

F Family
O Organization / Occupation
R Recreation
M Message
I   In-dept interest
N New Technology or New Thought Leadership
G Global Issue

Here are some questions you could potentially use within **F,O,R** and, we will let you know what you should do for **M** as well. We always start by asking the broadest question. Then depending on the person›s answers, you will drill down to the next question. Remember, this is a conversation, not an interrogation, especially on a call.

Family: This is general for where they grew up, kids, etc. Some people love to talk about family, and some don't and if they don't move on to the next category.

Where did you grow up?
Do you come from a large family?
Where are all the places/cities/countries you've lived ... Etc.

Organization/Occupation: This is the general category for exploring career and professional experiences. In all categories, we want to start broad and then narrow down.

In which industry do you work?
Which organization do you work for?
What function have you spent the most time?
What is your current role?

Recreation: This is where many like to share their interest or hobbies or whatever they have just completed that was interesting to them - a trip, something they made, or a half marathon they ran. All you have to do is ask: -

What do you do in your spare time?
Or what do you do for fun?

One of the things you might want to realize is you do not have to know or be an expert about their topic i.e., If they like golf and you are not a golfer. You say up front; I am not a golfer but really interested to learn how did you get started?

Message: Most people normally say thank you, hope to see you around soon or great speaking with you. Well, if everyone says that, then you are just like everyone else. Listen to pay attention, and here is where you summarize in one crisp line what they talked about the most or what they were most passionate about and give it back to them right before you disengage or leave. it will show you were listening.

I loved your story about your hiking adventure. I wish I were as brave as you.
Your daughter has a fantastic gift for the violin – you must be really proud of her.

In-dept interest, New Technology or New Thought Leadership, or Global Issue.

In case a senior leader turns to you and says, "what are you interested in?" you cannot go "mmm..." that is a clue you are just thinking about it. It would help if you had something exciting and ready to share in either of these three topics.

How **GOOD** am I at this facet?

_____

_____

_____

_____

What more do I need to do to be **GREAT** at this facet?

_____

_____

_____

_____

Facet #4 Gains Trust

Developing trust is one of the fundamental skills in any relationship you may have in life. The truth about trust is that it takes time
or multiple occasions that you deliver on your word that ultimately builds trust. It is also an element that can be lost very quickly. As
the saying goes, "It takes years to build up trust and only seconds
to destroy it." In terms of business relationships, however, gaining
trust has three main elements:

1) *Delivering Results.* When you follow through with a
   promise or meet (and exceed) expectations, people learn
   to trust and rely on you.

2) *Building Relationships.* In order to have trust, you first
   have to form real relationships. This takes some time, so
   be patient and work on getting to know people at all levels
   of your organization, especially if they are not in the same
   location or region.

3) *Showing Concern.* As I've mentioned before, people can tell
   when you're putting on a façade or being fake, so practice
   building sincere relationships by showing genuine regard
   for other people's feelings and points of concern.

Why is this facet important? Trust is the basis of all business
inter- actions; and in fact, it is the basis of any human interaction.
"Can I really trust this person to deliver on his promises or plans?"
is always in the back of our minds. It is the same from a customer's
view point of view: "Can this company I have chosen be trusted
enough to deliver what they promised?" You earn trust by focusing on all three of the above elements, which will then increase
your ability to establish trust within and outside the organization.

How **GOOD** am I at this facet?

_____

_____

_____

_____

_____

_____

What more do I need to do to be **GREAT** at this facet?

_____

_____

_____

_____

_____

_____

> **"Trust is a skill, one that is an aspect of virtually all human practices, cultures, and relationships."**
>
> **-Robert C. Solomon**

Facet #5
Provides Direct Feedback

This is an often-overlooked element of developing an Executive Mindset because, well, not many of us really feel comfortable doing it. Providing feedback to peers and even to superiors requires you to push back with appropriate assertiveness. This can be challenging to do and requires the proper timing, tone, and word choices. But it must be done. Here are two ways to push back in a way that will be well received:

1) *Share any negative news early.* If you have a POC(Point of Concern) or a problem, don't wait until too far along in the process when more effort (and emotion) is likely to be involved.

2) *Provide sensitive feedback.* As the adage goes: It's not what you say, it's how you say it. This couldn't be truer when it comes to providing feedback. Choose your words carefully and be aware of how you come across.

When providing your POC during meetings or in one-on-one discussions, here are a few ways to start and examples of each:

a) **Interject Professionally**

"Is it ok if I share some feedback with you?"

"Is it alright to share what our customers are saying?" "Is it ok to voice a slightly different view on this issue?"

b) **Thank the Person and State Your POC**

"I like your idea. However, have you considered that this may have happened?"

"That's great. Do we know that results will be guaranteed?"

"Wow, that is brilliant. Do we have time to consider another alterative that our competitors are using?"

c) State the Problem and Suggest Alternatives

"Jeff, this just happened. I can suggest two things we could do... What do you think?"

"Kim, I am sorry I misjudged the impact of the... I have these options to get it right... What do you think?"

"Jeremy, the item we were expecting did not arrive on time. I have two back up plans... What do you suggest?"

The impact of these alternatives depends on your tone, timing, and intention. People will know if you want to sincerely provide options or you simply want to shoot down their ideas. If you tell your leaders something went wrong, then don't just be a naysayer—instead, provide a solution. Of course, I am not talking about performance feedback discussions with your team members; that is a different discussion altogether. Rather, the suggestions above are more for discussions on business choices with your boss or senior leadership.

Why is this facet important? Most of the time, it's when you re- solve a problem that you really get noticed. You just need to do the prep work required to provide solutions and not just throw the problem back at your boss. Leaders want others who can solve problems—plain and simple. We all know that we can get better at this; it comes with practice, just as the other facets do.

Remember that in many cultures, getting feedback (even negative news) is expected and usually wanted early in the process. So figure out what the preference is in your company. Most of the time it is an individual leader's preference, so determine which of your leaders sets the tone for feedback timing. You have to know how "Rome" wants their "bad news" and then decide to get comfortable providing it this way. We tell our participants in our programs; your message is going to be viewed three ways, was it Positive, Neutral, or Negative. I hope you are not overly Negative all the time. We suggest if you're communicating to your

5% audience, keep it at least neutral. You don't need to avoid the issue but say it more positively. And if you are on the phone, your tone is even more important now.

QUESTIONS COULD DETERMINE YOUR CAREER

A friend of mine was the MD for a global recruitment firm in Singapore, and his boss' boss Patricia, held their regional kick-off meeting in their beautiful boardroom overlooking the sea.

When it was about 4.00 pm, Patricia asked to have the other staff in the office come in to listen to her announcement about the new program. After the short presentation, like all good leaders, she asked, "Any questions?"

My friend related; then, my staff, John, shot his hand up, and asked, "Since we had tried this last year and the year before and it failed, what makes you think it will be successful this time?"

Patricia gave a cursory reply, "If you don't try, you won't know."

Then I had a relatively new hire, Sandra, who asked, "Pat, I read in our intranet and newsletters that you had quite a few successes rolling out this new program with some of our global clients. Can you tell us how you did it?"

Patricia gave a long and illustrious answer. If it were not for the end of the day, she would have gone on.

**Make a guess, six months later, who got fired
and who got a promotion?**

How **GOOD** am I at this facet?

_____

_____

_____

_____

_____

_____

What more do I need to do to be **GREAT** at this facet?

_____

_____

_____

_____

_____

_____

> **If you never step out of your**
> **_Comfort Zone and into the 5% Zone,_**
> **you will not get to where you**
> **want to be in your business or life.**

Facet #6
Takes Ownership

Taking ownership in an effective manner that gets you noticed involves several major aspects:

1) *Show initiative.* This can include suggesting new ideas and picking up the slack where others on your team seem to be more hesitant.

2) *Readily lead projects.* You can't be afraid of stepping up and becoming the leader or project manager on an important task. In fact, when it's done right, there's no better way to get noticed. But remember that when you are the leader, blame tends to fall on your shoulders. When this happens, don't make excuses—find solutions.

3) *Willingly participate on teams.* You can't lead every time. Sometimes the most appropriate way to contribute is to be a solid team member.

Why is this facet important? Out of all seven facets, this one came out on top with the leaders I've interviewed over the years as the most desirable (and most lacking) facet. Companies both large and small constantly have new projects, initiatives, rollouts, and community events; and someone has to be in charge of these. So when leadership looks around for someone to lead, do you readily put your hand up or hide behind someone else? Yes, I'm sure you have your reasons for why you are not the right person. It's not the right time (you're too busy), or you're too new. Or maybe you've "done this before," and you think it's time to let someone else take the lead.

Leaders will eventually appoint someone, but I guarantee you they would prefer for someone to step up and take charge. So you have to figure out if that project, initiative, or committee is on your 5% list. If it is, your hand should go up fast. Being proactive is one surefire way to stand head-and-shoulders above the others. Ro- mans are looking for other Romans, and leaders are looking for other leaders who want to lead. The question is, are you that per- son now or in the future?

How **GOOD** am I at this facet?

_____

_____

_____

_____

_____

What more do I need to do to be **GREAT** at this facet?

_____

_____

_____

_____

"Sometimes, in organizations, we regret the chances we didn't take, the relationships we didn't take the time to build, and the decisions we took too long to make."

Stephen Krempl

Facet #7
Coaches and Recognizes Others

This is a facet that will definitely set you apart from your competition. If you can find ways to effectively help others achieve their goals, executives at all levels of your organization will take notice. In order to successfully do this, you must be willing to:

1) Guide and mentor team members (this includes people at and below—and even occasionally above—your level).

2) Recognize and reward the efforts of others openly. Don't be afraid to point out the contributions of others and praise them for it.

Everyone loves to be recognized for his or her efforts, ideas, or contributions. So the question is how much are you doing this for others? Do you ever thank a supervisor for something he did that stood out to you? The old Ken Blanchard advice still applies: "Catch someone doing something right."

Many leaders will tell you that they got where they are today be- cause someone took interest in their development or took them under their wing. Who can you help develop or take under your wing to help them achieve their goals? I know some of you may not feel comfort- able giving praise to others or receiving praise in public, but you must start picking this up as a good habit if you want to stand out.

Why is this facet important?

These three leaders sum it up best:

- "Recognition is the greatest motivator." -*Gerard C. Eakedale*
- "People may take a job for more money, but they often leave it for more recognition." -*Bob Nelson*
- "People often say that motivation doesn't last. Well, neither does bathing—that's why we recommend it daily." -*Zig Ziglar*

One final and important note: The most effective coaching and recognition come when it is planned. You can choose to do it spontaneously, but chances are you will be too busy. So, plan when, where, and what you are going to do at your next opportunity.

How **GOOD** am I at this facet?

_____

_____

_____

_____

_____

What more do I need to do to be **GREAT** at this facet?

_____

_____

_____

_____

_____

The Change Response Cycle and GEM

You're armed with some great ammunition so far—you know the 7 Facets of GEM and how they are the essential elements of the 5% Zone. There are three other critical areas that work right alongside the 7 Facets. We learned these three elements when I introduced the Response Cycle in a previous section. As a reminder, The Response Cycle and its three elements look like this:

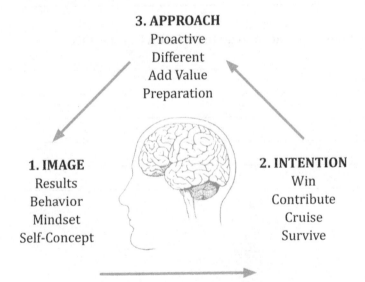

3. APPROACH
Proactive
Different
Add Value
Preparation

1. IMAGE
Results
Behavior
Mindset
Self-Concept

2. INTENTION
Win
Contribute
Cruise
Survive

THE RESPONSE CYCLE

1) The **Image** you have of yourself affects your...

2) **Intention** or how you handle your job, which in turn determines your...

3) **Approach** and the effort that you put into a situation Now we'll go into a little more detail for each aspect of the cycle:

1. Image

Your *self-concept* is how you see yourself, which was created early in your life by the influences of those people closest to you. Growing up, your family helped mold the way you now see yourself. In school, you were shaped by how your teachers and friends responded to you. This self-concept affects your *mindset*, which in turn affects your *behavior*, which then affects your *results*. Your results will rarely exceed your self-concept. So, figure out how to improve your self-concept from within, and then go after whatever you want.

2. Intention

Your self-image then determines the intention you have in work and life, represented by the Behavioral Approach Pyramid that we discussed earlier that looks like this:

BEHAVIORAL APPROACH PYRAMID

Some individuals have made an art out of justifying why they are "survivors" or "cruisers." Others try to contribute or win, but they may not know exactly what is stopping them. Ultimately, there is no right or wrong approach or intention—it really all depends on what you want from your career. Many people are content with where they are and what they are doing. But remember, my focus is not on them; my focus is on those who want to stand out.

When you were in school and you wanted to make an A, did that require making more effort than the kids who were content with all C's? *Of course.* It's all about your situation—some of us had to get good grades in order to maintain a GPA that was high enough to keep a scholarship, while others did it to satisfy their parents, and others were just smart.

What is your reason for wanting to *win* in your organization?

Are you prepared to make the "little changes" to get there?

3. Approach

If you know where you want results and you've chosen your intention, the next step is approach. This involves selecting those activities that will fall within your 5% Zone and then choosing one or more of these four ways to stand out:

1) Be Proactive
2) Be Different
3) Add Value
4) Be Prepared

In every situation (especially the 5% situations), you need to think about how you can add value, be original, and proactively solve problems. After all, these are the reasons you were hired in the first place.

However, in many cases, you can't do this unless you are prepared. Let's say you have to prepare for a meeting on ways to improve efficiency within your department. You determine this is a 5% meeting. You decide to research what other companies are doing and call a few friends to ask what their companies have done in similar situations. In other words, you do research (aka PREPARE) so that you can ADD VALUE to the next meeting by providing that information to others. This is the essence of how you stand out from your peers.

You could attend the meeting without preparing, but then you will just be a part of the crowd. So if you determine that your intention is to contribute or win, then the only way to do this is to be more prepared than the others. If the topic is in an area that you love, then you may already have a leg up. Either way, a little prep-work goes a long way. Pay attention to what's going on in the industry with regards to your topic or get information from your network.

If you really want to get ready, you may even have someone do some preliminary research for you. There are many companies on the Internet that provide this service, and it is often surprisingly affordable. Such efforts will enable you to walk in a lot more prepared and have real options to stand out from your competition.

> **"Be prepared, work hard, and hope for a little luck. Recognize that the harder you work and the better prepared you are, the more luck you might have."**
>
> *-Ed Bradley*

How Good Are You?

Before we continue learning more about the 5% Zone, it will be helpful to rate yourself to determine where you are right now and where your focus should be. For example, if you are really strong at communicating with confidence but find yourself lacking in coaching and feedback, that might be the best place for you to initially focus your 5% conscious efforts to improve. Write down a score from 1 to 10 for each of the categories below that reflects how you feel about these attributes (1 meaning least effective to 10 being absolutely great at it):

The 7 Facets of GEM

_____ ARTICULATES POINT OF VIEW

_____ COMMUNICATES CONFIDENTLY

_____ BUILDS TRUST

_____ CONNECTS PERSONALLY ON ALL LEVELS

_____ PROVIDES DIRECT FEEDBACK

_____ TAKES OWNERSHIP

_____ COACHES AND RECOGNIZES

Next, score yourself on a 1 to 10 scale for the focal point of the GEM Differentiator, the ways you can stand out (aka finding your 5% Zone):

Standing Out

_____ BE DIFFERENT

_____ IS PROACTIVE

_____ ADDS VALUE

_____ PREPARES WELL

By focusing on each of the facets at different times in your career, you can go from an employee who merely gets the job done to an integral, even indispensable, part of your organization. After all, that's the kind of person that executives will fight for to have on their team.

I RESIGN

This story was related to me, and you should pay attention to it. Ben was the HR VP for a large global electronics giant. He was relating this story to his mentor, and here is the conversation: -

Ben: I am fed up; I am going to resign.

Mentor: Why, what happened?

Ben: I am overworked and not appreciated, and my wife is complaining that the family hardly sees me. You see, when the Compensation and Benefits VP left, I took over that role, then the employee relations director resigned, and I took over that team, after that the L & D director left and I have taken over that team.

I am doing four jobs for the last 12 months, and I am tired. So when Susan (Global head of HR) comes next week, I am going to go in and tell her off. I am going to say I am doing all this work with no appreciation or compensation, and then I will tell her in her face - I am going to resign. Let's see what she is going to do now, and she will be up a creek?

Mentor: Ben, do you want to resign, you have been doing very well here? Do you have another job lined up?

Ben: NO

Mentor: Then why don't I suggest another strategy with Susan, and if nothing happens, you still can resign. You meet up with Susan and say:

Susan, I'd like to thank you for all the opportunities this organization has provided me over the time I have been here. When the compensation and benefits person left – I learned about Comp and Ben, when the Employee Relations director left, I had so much more exposure to the unions, and when the L & D person left, I was able to take charge of Employee Development. I am such a lucky person, no one in this company has had so many experiences in this sort a time. But because I am holding all these four roles, my family has seen less of me, and I must put them first. So, I have to resign regrettably.

Ben: OK, I will try that approach.

Fast Forward: After hearing Ben's message, Susan immediately acknowledged the situation, sent over some temporary resources to help. Not only that, that year, Ben was nominated and won the CEO's award, and he and his wife were flown to Florida to receive the award.

You can complain and be negative or you can learn to express your experience differently – your choice.

"You can stand on topof a rock or hide under it— it's your choice."

—STEPHEN KREMPL

Part IV

MAKING THE SWITCH

The 5% Switch Framework

In today's competitive local and global marketplace, your ability to stand out no matter where you are in your career is critical—and it's the key to your success. Because of the global nature of modern business, there is not only competition from your college peers or organizational peers, but also from people who travel the world in search of jobs, fame, and fortune. And guess what? Many of them are prepared to do what some "locals" are not prepared to do. They seem to be hungrier for success, determined to make a better life for themselves and their families, and are willing to work harder than others.

Whether you are interviewing for a new job, just starting out, in middle management, or presenting to the executive team, maybe it seems like there is something more you can do, but for reasons perhaps unknown, you always hold yourself back. Finding your 5% Zone can change that; and using "cues" is one way to help you make the *switch* to the 5% Zone.

Take a look at what I call the **5% Switch Framework** in the following table. The table is composed of the different kind of "cues" that you can incorporate into your life. These cues—whether they are Phrase, Physical, Picture, or Piece of Music —all serve one purpose. When you are faced with a situation where you need to bring something extra to the table, these cues can be the catalyst or the reminder to you that "this is a 5% moment." Look at the table for examples of each kind of cue:

5% SWITCH FRAMEWORK

Type of Cue	Example	Effect
Phrase	Positive Phrase: Lets Go! Speak Up! Just do it!	The words get you pumped up to stand out.
Picture or Visual Cue	Picture: Family Pic, Sun Rise, Audience Clapping	Seeing it reminds you of your vision or mission
Physical Cue	Squeeze fist, snap finger, Clasp both hands	This reminds you of your potential and greatness.
Piece of Music	A tune from favorite song or jingle	The song gets you pumped and motivated.

Making the switch is first about finding a type of "cue" (or cues) that works for you. Start thinking about what cues best motivate you to change your thoughts or actions. Those cues can be visual, mental, physical, or anything in between.

Take a moment and write down a cue or cues that get you pumped up and into your 5 % Zone:

Phrase: _____

Picture: _____

Physical: _____

Piece of Music: _____

My mission is to challenge people to increase their capability to communicate confidently, connect more personally, and stand out. But many people have two responses to this challenge that seem to stop them in their tracks. Their responses sound something like this:

1) "Well Stephen, I already know that."

2) "But Stephen, you don't understand. My situation is different..." ("My company is different..." "My customers are different..." "You just don't understand the type of tyrannical boss I have...")

Sure, we all have our reasons from time to time, but when you say those kinds of statements, you shut your mind off from exploring possibilities or seeing things in different ways. Stop sabotaging yourself and give yourself a chance to believe you *can* do it. One way to start doing this is by using the types of cues demonstrated in the 5% Switch Framework. Too many times we use our backgrounds and our past as an excuse not to stand out. We are here to live for today and prepare for the years to come—so let go and move on.

Becoming Aware of Your 5%

Are you aware that you probably aren't doing enough of what it takes to stand out? And are you aware that each and every one of you has a zone that you may have never operated from that can make all the difference? If you don't first recognize and acknowledge there is a problem or need for improvement, your mind simply won't allow you to take the necessary steps to improve. As I mentioned in the previous section, using cues is a great way to start training yourself when it's time to find your 5% Zone. Ultimately, it's plain and simple: Under- stand what you need to do, practice until it becomes natural, and success will be drawn to you when the time is right.

Here is a great analogy that my friend Larry Crain (of Release Technique fame) uses: *If you are looking for new answers, you can't find them by going back to the same old filing cabinet when there is nothing inside or the information in it hasn't changed.*

Why do you keep going back to the same file? And even more importantly, what are you saying to yourself that makes you go looking for new answers in old places? I've got a tip for you: Don't allow your mind to continue telling you that there is something useful in those old files. It's time to stop tricking yourself into returning to the dried up well (and thus your same old routine).

> **You need to find new content for the file.
> Otherwise, you keep using
> the same old crap.**

TIME OUT! BOX

Write down what you said to yourself as you read the paragraphs above:

_____

_____

_____

_____

_____

_____

_____

Now choose a cue or cues that you believe will get you to your 5% Zone and help break you out of the habit of using the old files:

Phrase: _____

_____

Physical: _____

_____

Picture: _____

_____

Piece of Music: _____

_____

I facilitate a program called Advanced Presentations, and one of the involvement techniques I teach when delivering technical presentations is the art of "Asking Questions." Sure, it seems obvious when you hear it or read it in a book, and before I demonstrate the technique in class, many people say (most likely in a whiney voice):

"Well Stephen, of course I tried asking questions, but it doesn't work. Nobody answers any of my questions when I ask the audience. I won't ask questions again. It's a waste of time."

My response to this is usually something like, "Hmm, that's odd. I've never had that problem myself. So, how come *you* do?" When I dig a little deeper and ask them the questions found in the box below, I usually find that they had no idea why asking questions didn't work for them. Here is what I ask:

1) Do you know how to construct a proper question to get the expected response?

2) Do you know that there are actually *eight* types of questions?

3) Do you know that there many ways to get responses, even if people don't respond the first time?

I soon find that they hadn't even rehearsed their audiences! How can you believe a technique to be lousy if you don't practice it? But as the saying goes, if your only tool is a hammer, then everything looks like a nail. Well I don't know about you, but I don't want to be a one-trick pony, which is why I prefer to use a different tool—a Swiss Army knife—that can cut, knock, drill, pound, glue, staple, and heck, even do your laundry. When you have more tools at your disposal, all you have to do is choose another gadget to use if the first one or two you try doesn't work for your specific purpose.

Once I teach the correct way to ask questions in my workshop, then I have the participants practice the technique. As you might expect, they usually get it wrong the first time because they've never done it properly before with guidance and feedback. But soon they learn, and it no longer seems difficult or useless. No one had ever shown them what to focus on to make the technique more effective. After practice, their response becomes (in a much less whiney voice):

"Ooh, I didn't know that was what I needed to do."

Well, now they do. And that is why recognizing your habitual LV statements that you use to hold you back is so crucial. Once you are aware of those statements, you can consciously switch into the 5% Zone where you can begin to fill a whole new filing cabinet full of fresh ideas, thoughts, and actions.

Remember, I don't want to change your 95%. I'm only interested in your 5% moments. But it is important to know what your 95% is saying to you that may be holding you back. This can be especially crucial in your 1% moments—the really big moments in life (like when you have to present to your boss' boss, secure a large account with a huge new customer, or meet your future mother-in-law for the first time).

THINK LIKE A CHAMPION

Who is the fastest 100-meter runner in the world? Usain Bolt. Do you think Usain Bolt steps up to the blocks thinking, "Shoot, I hope I don't screw this up! Please don't let me screw this up. Let me get to my best. Man, I really hope I don't screw this up." Do you think that is what is going through his mind?

He is probably saying something more like this: "I'm going to blow these guys away. I'm the fastest in the world. In fact, I'm going to break records. I've just got to focus." Well, whether you're on an Olympic track or in the corporate arena, it doesn't matter. What you are saying to yourself over and over again will become your reality. What is your 5% difference?

Preparing For 5% Situations

> ## A MISSED 1% MOMENT
>
> You step into the elevator to find that it's just you and your CEO. You say, "Good morning," and she replies, "Oh hi, how are you? What are you working on these days?"
>
> The chatter inside your head starts immediately:
>
> *"Gosh, I hope I don't screw this up."*
>
> *"Uh, uh, your name idiot, tell her your name!"*
>
> *"Should I tell her about my department, my specific project, or which division I'm in?"*
>
> *"Oh, and I should mention my boss' name so she knows... or ooh maybe I need to..."*
>
> Ding! She walks out at her floor, and all you managed to get out was your name and a decent handshake. You just missed your 1% opportunity to make your CEO say, "Man, I wish I had a few more sharp, confident people like that around in the organization."

Don't let your LV 2 hijack your brain in critical situations or you will find yourself in a similar situation to this unfortunate elevator passenger and miss a key 5% (or in his case, 1%) opportunity. In the web version of my GEM program, you can practice how to do this in the privacy of your own space if you have not attended a live GEM class or used any of the other resources. (Go to my website for more information on this: www.stephenkrempl.com.)

I once watched a post-game interview after the Olympics gold medal game in women's soccer, and the goalkeeper of the winning team said something I really liked. Her save in the final few seconds won the game for the team. When asked how she prepared for this critical moment, she said: "I practice diving to the right and left at least 300 times a day, so I know how to do it. When the opportunity presented itself in this game, I said to myself, *you've done this before; it's your time.* And I instinctively knew what to do."

How prepared are you for your 5% opportunities? How many times do you practice? How are you going to make the save, hit the proverbial ball out of the park, or throw the perfect pass if you don't practice? Practice engaging an audience, rehearse some great comeback lines for any situation, work on gaining trust, and share your point of view confidently.

TIME OUT! BOX

List 5% situations that you should be preparing for today:

_____

_____

Which of those situations do you need to practice for first?

_____

What do you need to practice?

_____

Who can help you review your practice?

_____

There may be times when you did decide to step up to the plate but then backed off your idea, project, or new practice because someone else told you that they tried it and it didn't work. Your 95% self immediately agreed that it was a stupid idea in the first place and said:

"Yep I thought so. You can't do that. Boy, they are so right."

Don't get me wrong—sometimes it's important to get other people's perspectives on a new idea or venture. I frequently consult with other people to learn from their experiences and points of view. But before you blindly believe what someone says, you need to find out a little more about their experience and how they came to that conclusion.

Here are some great questions to ask that will check if their points of view needs are valid for you and your idea:

Exactly what did you try and with whom?

_____

_____

How many times did you try it?

_____

Who did you learn that from and what results did that person (or you) get?

_____

_____

_____

_____

_____

_____

After you ask these questions and find out more about their specific experiences, it could be that they wrongly applied a few key techniques or have some preconceived notions and thoughts that are even more biased than yours.

The point is: Don't ever stop doing something just because someone tells you to! Do your homework and find out more.

Turning on the Switch

Whether it is from a self-introduction, sharing your POV, or communicating your message, you must ensure you are different enough so that those around you remember your comments and your message; and "cues" can be the key to this. Let's review the 5% Switch Framework with a column added that contains examples of each kind of cue:

5% SWITCH FRAMEWORK

Type of Cue	Type	Effect	Examples
Phrase	Positive Phrase, Motivational Words	The words get you pumped up and ready to stand out.	"You're on" "You are great" "It's your 5% time"
Physical	Action, Gesture or Anchor	This reminds you of your potential and greatness.	Squeezing your fist or tapping your feet 3 times
Picture	Picture or Object of Value or Meaning	Seeing it reminds you of your vision or mission.	Picture on cell- phone, object you keep in your office
Piece of Music	A tune from favorite song or jingle	The tune gets you going and motivated.	Play in your head Sing to yourself Listen to song

Cues are the solution for turning on the switch, finding your 5% Zone, and standing out; but if you find one cue is not enough to get you to your 5% Zone, then you could try a combination of multiple cues. For example, you could use a Physical Cue (like squeezing your fist) while if you use a Phrase (like saying to yourself "You're On") while you employ a Musical Cue or Piece of Music (like listening to the theme song to *Rocky* as you raise your hands over your head). This may sound like a lot, but in reality all of this will only take you a few seconds.

Read the story in the following box as you think about what cues may have been useful to the colleague from China:

SPEAK UP!

A *Fortune 100* executive invited a colleague from China to accompany him to a meeting at his company's corporate headquarters in the U.S. On the second day the executive's boss, an American, asked the executive in jest, *"Who is that guy over there? He tries to blend in with the furniture, doesn't say a word, and is just taking a lot of notes."* Is he a spy? Maybe if the colleague's English were not good, his silence would have been more acceptable (although his English was just fine). He was just being his 95% self (in this case 100%) and did not think it was important enough to make a few comments and share his thoughts and concerns—which he actually had— from his own market's perspective. Instead he retreated into his safe zone and crawled under a rock.

No one is asking you to say something simply for the sake of speaking, but if a company takes the trouble to fly you 7000 miles across the world, then you better come prepared to participate (even minimally). And this is just as important if you are participating in a Global Conference Call. Prepare questions to read aloud if you are afraid you will forget. You need to show people you are alive, which means it's time to turn on the switch!

Don't be the kind of person who goes to a company cocktail party, looks for a friend, hides in the corner, and then leaves after fifteen minutes. What a waste. Instead, turn on your switch and find a way to stand out.

"You are only as good as the person who comes before you or after you."

— STEPHEN KREMPL

Part V

FIVE TECHNIQUES FOR MAXIMIZING YOUR 5% ZONE

It's Time to Stand Out

You've got to turn on your switch using whatever cues work best for you. But once that switch is turned on, what's next? Well now it's time to stand out and be remembered! There are five specific techniques to maximize your 5% opportunities.

The five techniques are:

1) Increase Your Visibility

2) Raise Your Energy

3) Be Different

4) Add Value

5) Be Proactive

Now we'll discuss a few key points of each of the five techniques.

1. Increase Your Visibility

Use the following tactics to INCREASE YOUR VISIBILITY in any work or social situation:

- **Be at the right place at the right time.** Communicate the right things at the right place. This means you need to identify the most important meetings, company events, and external social gatherings or calls that you need to attend— and then let people know you are there!

- **Choose your commitments wisely.** If you are only going to attend a few events, carefully select which meetings or calls are of the most value to you, what problems are you going to help resolve, or what projects or tasks you are going to volunteer for.

- **Choose who you are wisely.** If you only have a few moments to socialize in a situation, don't just stand next to your best friend or peers from your department or say nothing on a call. Pick the superiors or the influencers that need to get to know you. Remember, this is not your normal 95%, so it may put you out of your comfort zone. But luckily, it won't be for very long.

- **Leverage the Call.** Use the first few minutes to "say something interesting." You can share an exciting piece of news, an inspiring customer story, fact, or result. Don't join the call and then start to think about what to say. It will be a little too late at that point to stand out.

- **Work the room.** Use the first fifteen minutes to "work the room." This could even mean that you make the rounds to just say "hi" to key people at the event. If it's your tendency to hide at parties or events, you can go into hiding mode only after you've let the right people know you are there.

- **Use the proper conversation tools.** When you are having a conversation with key people, insincerity is usually easily detected. Therefore, you must actually listen to what people are saying. That way, your responses will be both relevant and considerate. Practice striking up conversations with all types of people.

2. Raise Your Energy

Use the following tactics to RAISE YOUR ENERGY in any work or social situation:

- **Gauge your own natural energy level.** Learn your own natural energy levels (where you normally operate) so that you know the difference between your 0%, 25%, 50%, 75%, 100%, and 125% energy levels. Then you can determine when the right times are to raise your "natural" or default level in special situations.

- **Recognize the 95% triggers (and don't be a slave to them).** We all have some trigger or triggers that cause our energy levels to increase. For example, some people say, "I'm not a morning person. I need my coffee before I can get going." I'm sure that is correct 95% of time, but what happens if your alarm did not go off and you have an important meeting in fifteen minutes? What happens when you need to catch an early flight—how many of us can wake up instantly for that? This is a learned behavior, so you must recognize how to turn on your switch—with or without your trigger.

- **Know how to get to 100%—quickly.** If you know you normally operate at about 50% energy, practice turning on your switch from 50% immediately to 100%. This will come in handy if you are suddenly asked to stand up and speak at a meeting or an event (and you were not expecting to). You never want people to think you're a "boring" speaker, and the only way to assure you don't get labeled as such is to keep your energy level high in front of any group – in person or virtually.

3. Be Different

Use the following tactics to BE DIFFERENT in any work or social situation:

- **Look for ways to distinguish yourself and stand out.** If you hide in the crowd and keep your opinions to yourself, no one will ever know you. If your only contribution at meetings is to say, "I agree," then you simply won't be remembered. At that point, you're really just a warm body or a name on call list. Remember, you can hide under the rock or stand on the rock and be noticed.

- **Don't be a PIN.** I'm not asking you to be the kind of per-son who comments all the time or someone who constantly asks questions and raises a hand every five minutes. In fact, that approach usually has a negative effect. When those people say, "Can I say something?" everyone just rolls their eyes. Yet the only one who does not seem to pick up on this is that person. That person is what I call a "Pain In the Neck" (PIN)—and some are pains in lower places than the neck.

- **Pay attention to those before you.** Pay particular attention to the person who speaks right before you to ensure that you don't do exactly the same things, say the same phrases, or have nothing to add more than "me too." This includes using the phrase "I agree" anytime someone says something. You can agree with people and let them know on occasion, but not all the time—and when you do, add your own POV.

- **Use setup statements.** Try some different attention getting statements like, "Great point, Kim, and my take on that is..." Then give your POV and add real value to the discussion. These setup statements, which are statements you say right before you state your POV, are meant to draw attention to you before you make your point.

AUTHENTICALLY NEGATIVE.

During a Q & A session, a participant asked: "I get the 5% message, but we have been told to be authentic, so what is your opinion about that?"

I answered yes, we must be authentic within our roles, i.e., Authentic leader, parent, or friend. (do we act the same way for each of those roles probably not). We all play different roles, and you must be true to yourself, know your principles, and then articulate them as neutrally or positively as you can in those 5% situations.

Many people make the mistake of thinking I am going to be authentic and tell it like it is, then the message comes out a little blunt and negative, and then think they are authentic. If you do that once or maybe twice, you may get away with it, but if you are negative all the time. Do you think senior management wants to hear negative? Don't get me wrong; you are not avoiding the issue, but senior leaders want people to show them how the problem is going to be solved, not complain about every single little detail about the problem and then say, "So what do we do now?"

Also, you have to be careful because the person you are complaining too, might have been the one that created the problem in the first place.

So do you want to be "Authentically Negative"?

4. Add Value

Use the following tactics to ADD VALUE in any work or social situation:

- **Contribute something new.** Have information, ideas, or suggestions that contribute to the discussion. Many times at assessment meetings or employee development discussions, leaders talk about an individual and use the phrase, "Sally always *adds value* to any discussion." In order to have that phrase associated with you, then you have to bring something new to the table.

- **Come prepared.** When you take the time to prepare or make an effort to participate in the conversation, to problem solve, or to volunteer, people will notice. Most people just show up and think that's enough. Sometimes that's okay. But know when it would be a good time to do some extra preparation.

- **ABC (Always Be Contributing).** There are other times to add value during the day in addition to formalized meetings. Keep this in mind during impromptu hallway discussions (or water cooler talk) or even in an email. Be ready to offer something useful at a moment's notice. For example, if you hear your boss mention that he doesn't know how to make a certain chart for a meeting—and you do—then speak up. Adding value will do wonders for you both now and in the future.

5. Be Proactive

Use the following tactics to BE PROACTIVE in any work or social situation:

- **Take the risk.** When you volunteer to speak or contribute first, this speaks volumes to your superiors about your drive, ability, and initiative. Be proactive by asking how you can help long before being asked.

- **Offer your assistance.** Offering your assistance in early phases such as project setup and information gathering is a great way to stand out. Don't wait for a problem or issue to arise before you step up. This is not hard to do if you are willing to occasionally spend a little extra time and energy.

- **Be ready to seize the moment when no else wants to.** Pick moments to have a "Hands up First" mentality. If you are in a group—whether it be 5 or 50 people—when the leader says, "Anyone have any questions?" don't let that be the first time you've thought about a response. You need to know at the start of the meeting what general questions or requests may arise and prepare ahead of time.

VOLUNTEER TO GET REMEMBERED

In my early days at Motorola, I volunteered to be on the opening committee for our new manufacturing facility. When it came to assigning each person something to do, I also volunteered to emcee the event, a role everyone avoided like the plague. But it was easy for me, and it also happened to be the most visible role—I got to greet everyone, and every person in the audience got to at least see and hear me. And by doing a good job, they remembered me.

When and Where Chart

With these five techniques, you've got the tools to find the 5% Zone and stay there for as long as you need to. Use the *When and Where Chart* below to identify the events where you want to practice the five techniques:

1. Increase Your Visibility

2. Raise Your Energy

3. Be Different

4. Add Value

5. Be Proactive

In the blanks provided in the table on the following page, briefly describe ways to accomplish each of the five techniques for your particular situations (meetings, events, social gatherings, etc.):

When And Where Chart

What else do you need to do to be remembered by more people in the organization?

EVENT	1._____	2._____	3._____
Increase Visibility			
Raise Energy			
Be Different			
Add Value			
Be Proactive			

"It's not where you start; it is where you decide you want to finish that sets you apart."

— STEPHEN KREMPL

Part VI

EXERCISE AND APPLICATION WORKSHEETS

Application Exercises to
Identify Your 5% Opportunities

No matter who you are or what you do, there are times when you need to stand out, communicate confidently, and connect with people. And now you know how the 5% Zone and GEM work together and how important those select opportunities can be. Obviously, not every meeting, presentation, or interaction is a 5% situation; but I want you to practice at every opportunity so that when the time comes you are ready and rehearsed.

It's now time to start identifying important situations that get you closer to your goals or solving a problem for your department or even your organization. I encourage you to complete each of these exercises.

You can never get enough practice!

ACTIVITY #1
Find Your 5% at Meetings and Conference Calls

Meetings are a part of our corporate lives, and yet sometimes I think we have far too many. I can remember a time when all I did was go from one meeting to another. When was I supposed to do my work??? But these meetings were critical to the way the organization functioned. So take some time and identify your 5% meetings.

One-on-One Meetings: Who are the key people that I absolutely need to make a good impression on in one-on-one meetings with them? (The correct answer is not "everyone.") Name the top three in the space below and what their impact is on you:

1. Meeting:

_____

_____

What more can you do?

_____

_____

_____

_____

Impact:

_____

_____

_____

_____

2. Meeting:

_____

_____

What more can you do?

_____

_____

_____

_____

_____

Impact:

_____

_____

_____

_____

_____

3. Meeting:

_____

_____

What more can you do?

_____

_____

_____

_____

_____

_____

Impact:

_____

_____

_____

_____

_____

_____

Small Team Meetings/Calls: These are meetings that occur either with- in your group or function versus those that are cross-functional or outside your group. Which meetings are important enough that   I need to make extra preparations, make positive contributions, and add value? (Again, don't say every meeting.) Name the three in the space below that are critical to you and what impact you can make at them:

1. Meeting:

_____

_____

What more can you do?

_____

_____

_____

_____

Impact:

_____

_____

_____

_____

_____

2. Meeting:

_____

_____

What more can you do?

_____

_____

_____

_____

_____

_____

_____

Impact:

_____

_____

_____

_____

_____

_____

3. Meeting:

_____

_____

What more can you do?

_____

_____

_____

_____

_____

_____

Impact:

_____

_____

_____

_____

_____

_____

Large Functional or Group Meetings/Calls: Your chances of becoming known or getting noticed start at the larger company or functional meetings. So which meetings does my function (or position) make it possible for me to organize and prepare for in order to make positive contributions? Name three in the space below where you feel you can make a real impression and what impact your contributions may have:

1. Meeting:

_____

_____

What more can you do?

_____

_____

_____

_____

_____

Impact:

_____

_____

_____

_____

_____

_____

2. Meeting:

_____

_____

What more can you do?

_____

_____

_____

_____

_____

_____

_____

Impact:

_____

_____

_____

_____

_____

_____

3. Meeting:

_____

_____

What more can you do?

_____

_____

_____

_____

_____

_____

Impact:

_____

_____

_____

_____

_____

_____

Large Company Meetings: Most companies have large team meetings, town hall, all hands, kick-off meetings, or end of year celebrations in which everyone attends. Which ones could you volunteer to help with to raise your visibility to upper and senior management? Name three below that you could contribute your skills or talents to and what impact your contributions could make:

1. Meeting:

_____

_____

What more can you do?

_____

_____

_____

_____

_____

Impact:

_____

_____

_____

_____

_____

_____

2. Meeting:

_____

_____

What more can you do?

_____

_____

_____

_____

_____

_____

Impact:

_____

_____

_____

_____

_____

_____

3. Meeting:

_____

_____

What more can you do?

_____

_____

_____

_____

_____

_____

Impact:

_____

_____

_____

_____

_____

_____

Conference Calls: Which conference calls do you participate in on a regular basis? Which ones could you participate in more purposefully—especially during the Q&A? Name four in the space below and what impact your speaking up may have:

1. Conference Call:

_____

_____

What more can you do?

_____

_____

_____

_____

_____

_____

Impact:

_____

_____

_____

_____

_____

_____

2. Conference Call:

_____

_____

What more can you do?

_____

_____

_____

_____

_____

_____

Impact:

_____

_____

_____

_____

_____

_____

3. Conference Call:

_____

_____

What more can you do?

_____

_____

_____

_____

_____

_____

Impact:

_____

_____

_____

_____

_____

ACTIVITY #2
Find Your 5% in Business Functions

Formal functions, informal functions, and networking meetings are activities that many find to be wastes of time or too time consuming. But these are the activities where you meet, greet, and get to know people on a different and more personal level. These meetings will also establish whether you are a broader leader who can hold your own at these events when everything under the sun may be discussed.

As you progress up the organization, the people who attend these events get more and more sophisticated, and you will need to be at your very best to stand out. Start practicing and getting comfortable with these functions; they are an important part of the global business world. So take some time and identify your 5% events and know what to say using FORMING.

Informal/ Socials/ Meals: Which informal meetings, lunches, or drink meetups do you want to join or initiate to help you build relationships. What if I work remotely, what are my plans within the organization and to find out more about specific individuals? Name the three individuals you are trying to build better relationships with and what impact a better relationship with these people can have on you and your business:

1. Individual:

_____

_____

What more can you do?

_____

_____

_____

_____

_____

_____

Impact:

_____

_____

_____

_____

_____

2. Individual:

_____

_____

What more can you do?

_____

_____

_____

_____

_____

_____

Impact:

_____

_____

_____

_____

_____

_____

3. Individual:

_____

_____

What more can you do?

_____

_____

_____

_____

_____

_____

Impact:

_____

_____

_____

_____

_____

_____

Formal/ Socials/ Meals: Which formal functions, dinners, or "wine downs" do you need to attend or be seen at to help you build relationships within the organization? Name three individuals who will be attending these formal functions with whom you are trying to build better relationships who can assist you in becoming better known or be more visible in the company:

1. Individual:

_____

_____

What more can you do?

_____

_____

_____

_____

_____

_____

Impact:

_____

_____

_____

_____

_____

_____

2. Individual:

_____

_____

What more can you do?

_____

_____

_____

_____

_____

_____

Impact:

_____

_____

_____

_____

_____

_____

3. Individual:

_____

_____

What more can you do?

_____

_____

_____

_____

_____

_____

Impact:

_____

_____

_____

_____

_____

Customer Meetings/Calls: Customers are the lifeblood of your organization. If you can create special relationships with key people inside your top customers' companies to increase your understanding or get market intelligence, it will greatly increase your value to your own organization. Name three customers that you want to connect with over the next few months or year to build better relationships. What impact will this relationship have on your business? Then pick the one that you will start with and mark YES next to that name: (Important note: Ensure you deliver on your promises that you have made during the meetings.)

1. Name of Customer:

_____

_____

What more can you do?

_____

_____

_____

_____

_____

_____

_____

Impact:

_____

_____

_____

_____

_____

2. Name of Customer:

_____

_____

What more can you do?

_____

_____

_____

_____

_____

Impact:

_____

_____

_____

_____

_____

_____

3. Name of Customer:

What more can you do?

Impact:

External/ Networking Groups: Which meetings, associations, or mastermind, Facebook, or LinkedIn groups do you need to join to expand your network outside the organization? These relationships could aid you in gathering market intelligence on what other companies are doing on a particular project or initiative. Name the three groups you want to join and pick one to spend the most time with for the year. Mark YES next to the one you want to choose for this year:

1. Group:

_____

_____

What more can you do?

_____

_____

_____

_____

_____

_____

Impact:

_____

_____

_____

_____

_____

_____

2. Group:

_____

_____

What more can you do?

_____

_____

_____

_____

_____

_____

Impact:

_____

_____

_____

_____

_____

_____

3. Group:

_____

_____

What more can you do?

_____

_____

_____

_____

_____

_____

Impact:

_____

_____

_____

_____

_____

_____

ACTIVITY #3
Find Your 5% at Unexpected or Unplanned Events

Sometimes things pop up that may catch a normal person off guard. But someone who focuses on the 7 Facets is always prepared. Here are a few situations to get you started, and you can add others for your particular needs. Below each one, list how you could best handle these situations in a way that will get you remembered:

1. Situation: Impromptu lunch with someone from HQ.

_____

_____

_____

_____

2. Situation: Chance meeting with CEO or Executive Team Member.

_____

_____

_____

_____

3. Situation: You get asked your POV on a controversial project.

_____

_____

_____

_____

4. Situation:

_____

_____

_____

_____

5. Situation:

_____

_____

_____

_____

6. Situation:

_____

_____

_____

_____

ACTIVITY #4
Find Your 1% Opportunities

Choose 3 things from all the activities that you listed on the previous pages that are the most important to you. These become your 1% activities (the events that you absolutely want to be prepared for).

The 1% Events that I must be ready for are:

1. _____

_____

_____

_____

2. _____

_____

_____

_____

3. _____

_____

_____

_____

ACTIVITY #5
Identify Your Little Voice (LV)

When it's all said and done, if you are the same as the person who comes before you or the one who comes after you, chances are you won't be remembered if that person is articulate and well prepared. So guess what...

> *You can't just be good.*
>
> *If you want to stand out, even being great may not cut it if your competition is well prepared and rehearsed.*
>
> *In your 5% situations, you might just have to be spectacular.*

Remember your competition at all times and never believe for a second that other people aren't comparing you to everyone else who's ever done your job.

Take this short quiz to determine if you're letting your LV2 speak for you (or simply shut you up) at meetings. When someone comes up with a great idea in a meeting, put a check mark next to all the phrases that you might say to yourself:

_____ I guess my idea is not that great - let me think this through more.

_____ What happens if my idea sounds stupid to others?

_____ Can this really work?

_____ What makes you an authority on this subject?

_____ What makes you the expert?

_____ I am going to look foolish if I speak up.

_____ What can I do to capture everyone's attention?

_____ Can I suggest another point of view?

_____ Just go for it.

Your Little Voice will always be there, and it will always tell you the things that it's been programmed to say over the years. As long as you know that and acknowledge that, there is no goal you cannot accomplish. I really don't care if you listen to your LV2 95% of the time. You just need to quiet it down 5% of the time.

Are you saying things that will help you or sabotage you? Are you aware of the phrases you use over and over again? And the real question: *Can you do something about it?*

The answer to that last question is obvious, but it is yours to decide. Be prepared to make a change 5% of the time to greatly enhance your career and your life. Rocks can be used to stand on or to hide under. So, decide to stand on the rocks and boulders that come your way. Practice the little things and learn the GEM behaviors, and you will surprise yourself with the levels of greatness you can achieve.

WITH THE RIGHT TOOLS, YOU CAN STAND OUT

I noticed two participants in one of my GEM sessions paying particular attention to everything I said and being *extremely* earnest during their practice time. During the break, I just had to ask them why they were so intense, and they replied that their CEO was coming to their country in two weeks to pay their office a visit and check things out. They really wanted to make sure the CEO knew who they were before he left.

So, I decided to help them along even further. During the class role-plays, I played the part of their CEO. I drilled them on the timing and phrasing of their questions and taught them how not to use "gotcha" questions. I also told them what to do if their CEO threw a question right back at them.

The real proof would *not* be that they could do it in class but that they actually could step up to the plate and do the things we practiced back in the "real world." I was later elated to hear they did ask their CEO some questions. More importantly, they surprised many people in the audience with the quality of their questions and the fact that they actually spoke up. They found their 5% Zone, and as for others in the audience, well, we all know what their LV2 must have been saying. The right tools, a little practice, and a little confidence go a long way in helping you stand out. They did—and so can you.

"To dream anything that you
want to dream. That's the beauty
of the human mind.

To do anything that you want
to do. That is the strength
of the human will.

To trust yourself to test your limits.
That is the courage to succeed."

— BERNARD EDMONDS

About the Author

Stephen Krempl is CEO of Krempl Communications International. As an international trainer, speaker, author and coach he had worked with thousands of leaders in over 30+ countries. His career spans 25 years' working for Fortune 500 companies, **Starbucks Coffee Company** where he was Chief Learning Officer (Seattle), **YUM Brands Inc**. VP of Yum University and Global Learning (Louisville), **PepsiCo** Restaurants International (Dallas) and **Motorola** (Singapore) He is an expert on how leaders can stand out and get noticed in their corporations even in an increasingly competitive global market place. He is the creator of the Global Executive Mindset (GEM) and Winning in the Work World (W3) programs. Stephen has also authored five books including: *The 5% Zone – How to Stand Out as a Global Executive* and is a Certified High-Performance Coach.

He is a high energy and engaging speaker who has spoken at multiple conferences and conventions around the world. Current area he speaks on :**The Impact of Artificial Intelligence on the Workforce – The Needs for Power Skills**

His has run training programs in many countries in Europe, Asia, and Middle East. Some of Stephen's clients include BNP

Paribas, Schneider Electric, VISA, BASF, Barclay's Bank, Applied Materials, Alcon, Qualcomm, UBS, OCBC, DBS, BOS, Kelly Services, CBRE, Monsanto, Hisense, ANZ, CB&I, FMCT, Telkom Indonesia, Mandiri Bank, Khazanah Nasional, Yum Brands, Ericsson, Fiserv, ASPAC, Fluke, Americana and Youth Olympics 2010 Organizing Committee.

His Global Executive Mindset(GEM) programs are offered through keynote speeches, in house and online programs that focus on developing high potential and future leaders especially minorities to get noticed in their organizations. He is now spreading this GEM message to universities, enabling students to understand what is expected of them and through an online curriculum called Winning in the Work World. For more information go to: www. WinningintheWorkWorld.com.

Prior to his current CEO role, Stephen was the VP of Global Learning at Starbucks Coffee Company. The role required the setting and implementation of an enterprise wide learning strategy for the 140,000 partners' 12,800 restaurants operating in 37 countries to enable the planned and systematic growth of the brand across the globe.

At YUM Brands Inc., Stephen was the VP of Yum University and Global Learning. This entailed taking care of the developmental needs of the top 3000 executives. YUM Brands operates 34,000 restaurants with 850,000 employees in over 100 countries for quick service restaurant brands KFC, Pizza Hut, Taco Bell, Long John Silver and A & W.

Stephen had also worked for Fortune 500 companies PepsiCo, Motorola including being a consultant at the Singapore Institute of Management. These senior training and education roles in these companies have enabled him to participate in the development and training of leader's globally.

For more information about Stephen and his organization and how your organization can participate in In-House or our Online GEM and Coaching sessions. Please visit his website at:

www.stephenkrempl.com

For additional information on our *online* and *classroom* training programs, please review the following pages.

Krempl Communications International LLC

Email: info@kremplcommunications.com
www.kremplcommunications.com

Winning in the Work World™ | 5% Zone
ONLINE Program for Current Professionals

10 micro-videos to instruct and inspirer with worksheets and skill practice videoswork-sheets and skill practice videose, worksheets, and skill practice videos

Incorporating a practical and highly effective GEM (Global Executive Mindset) model, GEM Online helps you develop a standout global mindset and overcome cultural barriers within your organization and industry. Through micro-video sessions and real-time feedback from both your peers and superiors,

W3 | 5% Zone Online shows you how to:

- Use the GEM Philosophy to stand out
- Connect personally at all levels
- Articulate your P.O.V. clearly
- Connect and communicate confidently
- Build trust with key stakeholders
- Provide direct feedback positively
- Coach and recognize others
- Develop a Personal Action Plan

W3 | 5% Zone is power packed with 10 micro-videos to maximize time for learning. It includes worksheets and skill practice videos to enhance what you learnt. Additional options are to include individual feedback and coaching, so participants can receive personalized advice and feedback to boost their career growth and success.

Winning in the Work World™ (W3) – ONLINE
Online Program for New Job Entrant
21 micro-videos to maximize time, worksheets, and skill practice videos

Incorporating the practical and highly effective content from both books, "You're Hired - Now What Do You Do?" and "The 5 % Zone" shows you know how to stand out and have the right mindset in your First Job through the 21 micro-video sessions and practice scenarios you.

W3 Online shows you :

- When to speak (and what to say) to your superiors in meetings
- How to create a positive impression when interacting with their team members
- How to generate energy and enthusiasm instantly
- How to connect with subordinates, peers, and superiors through appropriate communication at each level
- What employers want you to focus on in your new job
- And much more!

The six-module series is power-packed with 21 micro-videos to maximize learning time. Includes worksheets, and skill practice videos to reinforce learning. Additional options are to include individual feedback and coaching, so new job entrants can receive personalized advice and feedback to boost the

Workshop for Expat Managers
Getting Staff or Subordinates to Speak Up
Half-Day Workshop on How to Get Locals to Speak Up and
Participate in Your Meetings

Have you had the agonizing problem of not being able to get your staff to speak up at your meetings? Do you ask questions, only to get silence or even team members who pretend to write notes or answer a "sudden" important text or call? If you've faced any of these problems, let us show you in a short, quick, and effective session how you can minimize—if not eliminate—many of these problems with practical techniques that will make your life a lot easier.

Objectives:

At the end of the session, you will be able to:

1. Get your meetings to be more productive.
2. Enable two-way communications to take place.
3. Ensure everyone participates to the best of their abilities.
4. Understand cultural beliefs that cause these problems.
5. Develop your next meeting action plan.

Coaching Program for Executives and Managers
Achieve "Breakthrough" Behaviors for Standing Out, Communicating Confidently and Connecting Personally to Senior Management

Do you want to just cruise and survive in your organization or do you want to achieve breakthrough success for yourself? Acquire the skills and behaviors to make you Stand Out, Communicate Effectively, and Connect Personally as a Global Executive?

Objectives:

Our coaching program in either a 3 or a 6-session format will help you develop techniques to create:

1. Positive reframing and sharpening of the skills necessary to become an astute global executive.
2. Practice the mental discipline to make the changes needed to adopt and sustain these winning behaviors.
3. Behaviors that you need to transform and get to the next level.
4. Feedback on how you can make a difference in your organization.

5% Zone Workshops for Managers and Leaders

1-Day and 2-Day Workshops that will Make You STAND OUT to Senior Management.

Are you someone who achieves business results, but still lacks the presence to stand out to your executive team? Are you getting the attention you deserve from your global leaders with ease? Acquire these essential skills and behaviors to make you Stand Out, Communicate Effectively, and Connect Personally to senior leaders in your organization.

If you want to stand out in today's world either in person or online, then you will need to learn the 7 facets from the GEM model. The 1-Day Program includes 3 of the facets, while the 2-Day Program will provide you with all 7 facets.

Objectives:

In a highly interactive class, you will learn:

1. Understand the importance of GEM Philosophy and how to get into your 5% Zone.
2. To stand out and get noticed on a global stage whether in person or online.
3. Visibility Strategies that will get you Noticed.
4. Identify your cultural and or mental blocks that may be limiting your effectiveness.
5. Practice the facets scheduled for the workshop.

Other in-house programs in our curriculum include: -

— Business Story Telling
— Advanced Presentations
— GEM: Communicator
— GEM: Influencer
— Positively Negative
— Thinking at the Next Level

Krempl Communications International LLC

Email: info@kremplcommunications.com
www.kremplcommunications.com

Made in the USA
Monee, IL
22 October 2023

44999760R00105